AT WAR IN
KOREA

AT WAR IN
KOREA

GEORGE FORTY

Bonanza Books
New York

Previous page: An M4A3 tank of the 5th RCT, US Eighth Army, fires on Taejong-ni on the road to Chinju, during the offensive in that area, 9 August 1950.
US Army via Patton Museum

This 1985 edition is published by Bonanza Books, distributed by Crown Publishers, Inc., by arrangement with Hippocrene Books.

Manufactured in the United States of America

Library of Congress Cataloging in Publication Data

Forty, George.
  At war in Korea.

  Originally published: Shepperton, Surrey : I. Allan, 1982.
    Bibliography: p.
    1. Korean War, 1950–1953.
    I. Title.
DS918.F64   1985
951.9′043   84-18487
ISBN: 0-517-455889

h g f e d c b a

4

Acknowledgements

This is my seventh book in the 'at War' series and as with the others, I have tried deliberately to keep the accounts of the battles fought at unit and sub-unit level, because I feel that is the level to which the average individual can relate more easily than to the higher overall strategy. I have also tried to find as many personal accounts as possible and to tell the story of the Korean War through the eyes of those who actually did the fighting. In this connection, I would like to thank the following for all the kind and generous help I have received in the preparation of this book:

Establishments, units etc
The United Nations Organisation, both the London Information Centre and the Headquarters, New York; The Hellenic Embassy, London; The Embassy of the Grand Duchy of Luxembourg, London; The Royal Netherlands Embassy, London; The Royal Norwegian Embassy, London; The Swedish Embassy, London; The US Army Military History Institute; The US Army Audio-Visual; The United Services Organisation, World HQ; The US Army and Air Force Exchange Service; The Historical Branch, US Army; The Historical Branch, USMC; The Patton Museum of Cavalry and Armour; The Australian War Memorial; The National Defence HQ, Ottawa; Establissement Cinematographique et Photographique des Armees, Fort d'Ivry; Public Archives, Canada; RHQ, The Argyll & Sutherland Highlanders; RHQ, The Duke of Wellington's Regiment; RHQ, The Gloucestershire Regiment; RHQ, The Royal Tank Regiment; HQ NAAFI; HQ SKC: Gale & Polden Ltd; *Soldier* Magazine; The Imperial War Museum, Department of Photographs; The Ministry of Defence Library; The Royal United Services Institution Library; The National Association of Korean War Veterans.

Individuals
The late Lt-Col A. J. Barker; Mr D. Bool; Mr S. Dunstan; Mr A. P. Eagles; Capt H. B. Eaton; Lt-Col C. F. Eaton OBE; Lt-Col A. D. Fitzgerald MBE; Mr G. A. Granville; Col E. D. Harding DSO; Maj L. F. H. Kershaw DSO; Maj G. J. Mann; Col G. L. Neilson DSO; Dr Odd Oyen; Mr A. R. Owens; Mr F. E. Smith; Brig A. R. D. G Wilson CBE; Col Yong Kwon Chi, Defence Attache ROK Embassy, London.

Contents

951.9
F

Introduction

The United Nations Command in Korea was a completely revolutionary way in which to use armed force. Never before had the free nations of the world banded together to produce a navy, army and air force to go to the defence of a small country which had been invaded by an aggressively-minded neighbour. The major ground element of these forces was known as the United States Eighth Army; however, as you will read, it contained soldiers from many countries. It was formed with the purpose of halting the spread of Communism in Far East Asia by force of arms and, although one could well say that the outcome of the war was more of a 'stand-off' than a complete victory, at least the Republic of Korea still exists and was not swallowed up by its avaricious northern neighbour.

The Korean war was 'my war', and the adventure it brought made an exciting change from peacetime soldiering in the British Army of the Rhine. As a young tank officer, I commanded a troop of Centurions in support of two famous British infantry battalions of the Commonwealth Division — first the Black Watch and then the Duke of Wellington's Regiment. I was particularly happy to be in support of the latter, as both my father and brother had served with the Dukes. We were located on a thoroughly unpleasant feature known as the 'Bloody Hook', where the Chinese trenches were a few hundred yards away from our own. I had a fairly brief war, being wounded by a mortar bomb in

Below: The United Nations Security Council resolution of 7 July 1950, forms a backdrop to an American field gun crew as they bump over a dusty track somewhere in Korea. *United Nations, New York*

the May 1953 battle for the Hook, after only a few weeks in the line. However, that event did at least enable me to see other types of units — such as the now famous M A S H! A junior officer in the line during the static war of 1952-3 did not get much chance of sightseeing, being very much confined to his battalion area. Fortunately one of my five tanks was just inside the Turkish brigade sector, on our left flank, and, like many others, I also made useful contacts with neighbouring American units, which assisted bartering part of our beer ration for such delights as peanut butter and fruit juice. They were 'dry' in the line, so it was to our mutual advantage to exchange NAAFI and PX items. Occasionally we met soldiers of other nationalities, certainly we did so during the period which my regiment spent in reserve, and of course the Commonwealth Division was itself a wonderful mixture, so one did get the feeling of belonging to a truly international force. Like other UN soldiers I was deeply shocked by the poverty and squalor in and around the port of Pusan; I don't think I have ever seen people having to live in such conditions before or since, especially during the bitter winter weather, when in freezing conditions, refugees were struggling to stay alive in shanties composed only of flimsy cardboard boxes. The villagers and peasant population were luckier, being on the whole better fed and housed. They impressed me most of all by their inherent cheerfulness and the inventive use they made of the things we threw away — empty beer bottles, tins etc. No wonder they were able to make such a spectacular 'leap forward' in the last 20 years.

The combination of the static warfare conditions and the fact that the UN had virtual air supremacy meant that enormous camps grew up behind the front lines. Their large, painted signs had to be seen to be believed, as did the elaborate camp layouts, with whitened stones along the paths, etc, as each unit did its damndest to outdo the next for 'bull'. In the line of course it was a very different matter and conditions we lived under were far more like those my father experienced in the trenches of Gallipoli and Flanders than any other. The enemy showed himself to be a master of the art of camouflage, and although his frontline was so close to ours in the Hook sector, it was virtually impossible to detect his actual positions.

Unless one was actively connected with the Korean War, either serving there or knowing someone who was out there, the fighting had little impact on the daily life of the average person in the West, except

Above: United Nations plaque to men who fell in the war.
ROK Embassy, London

Left: 'Welcome UN Forces'. Lt-Col J. A. Dextraze, commanding the 2nd Royal 22e Regiment is greeted by local South Koreans, as the Canadian Brigade arrive at Pusan, May 1951.
Public Archives Canada DND SF-1456

when the occasional sensation hit the headlines. In any case it dragged on for so long that, after the first few months, most people were heartily sick of hearing about it, particularly as it came only five years after the end of World War 2. In retrospect, it is perhaps a pity that the West did not take a more active interest in the war, as it was one of the very few successful actions taken to stop the spread of Communism. Thirty years later, the Soviet Union has walked calmly into Afghanistan, in much the same way as North Korea invaded South Korea, but the West's reaction has been muted by comparison. To the cynical observer this would tend to suggest that the 72,500 men of the United Nations forces who were killed fighting in Korea, died in vain. In a tribute to his men, Gen Matthew B. Ridgway said that he believed that history would some day record that: 'the crest of the Communist wave of cold blooded aggression was broken against the arms and will to fight of the United Nations battle team in Korea . . .' Unfortunately, as Canute discovered, there is more than one wave in any ocean.

This book is but a small tribute from an ex-member of the 1st Commonwealth Division, United States Eighth Army, to all fellow Korean veterans all over the world, especially those who left their homelands to fight and did not return.

George Forty

Above: Main port buildings of Pusan. *George Forty*

Above right: Standard bearers meeting a troopship (*Empire Orwell***) at Pusan harbour. Flags are (l to r): ROK, USA, UN.** *George Forty*

Right: Troopships arriving at Pusan were met by an immaculate American Army band. *George Forty*

Below right: Author pictured outside his bunker on the Hook position. *George Forty*

8

The land and its people

To its people, Korea is known as *Chosen*, the 'Land of the Morning Calm'. Its western name of Korea is derived from the Koryo dynasty which lasted from AD 935 to 1392, and has an equally delightful literal translation, namely: 'Land of High Mountains and Sparkling Streams'. Beautiful though the country is, I'm sure that all those who served with the United Nations forces there will agree with the 'high mountains' part of that description! Wherever one walked there was yet another steep, jagged hill to be climbed. The total area of Korea is 85,200sq ml (compare with Great Britain — 88,950sq ml). In fact only about one fifth of the entire country is suitable for cultivation, rice being the staple crop. Located in the very heart of the Far East, the peninsula of Korea has long been of strategic importance and a prime target for would-be conquerors. It juts out from the Manchurian land mass and is approximately 525 miles long, varying in width between 125 and 200 miles. All round the coast are thousands of small islands. The northern border of Korea is bounded by two large rivers, the Yalu (also called the Amnok) and the Tumen (or Tuman). As the guide-book says: 'the climate of Korea is humid and continental. However, Korea has a pronounced rainy season in the summer and relatively dry winters. Throughout Korea the summers are hot . . . winters in the north are dry and cold; in the south the winters are relatively mild . . .' Ask an ex-UN soldier what the weather was like and he will probably tell you about sudden torrential downpours that soaked you to the skin in the summer and, above all, of the bitter, numbing cold of the winter when winds straight from the wastes of Manchuria brought the temperature down to 40° below, making even the simplest military task an effort if one was not properly clothed in full winter kit (and as some would also add almost downright impossible if one was!). Cold and heat are relative terms and must be compared with what an individual is used to, but I doubt if any of the thousands of

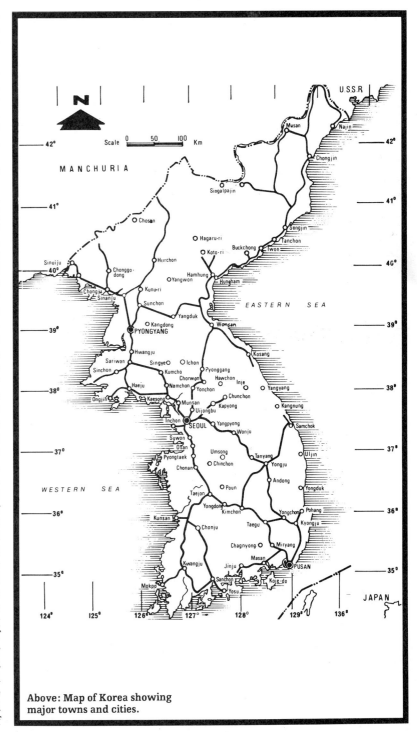

Above: Map of Korea showing major towns and cities.

refugees who existed in cardboard packing cases in the slums of Pusan ever described the climate as being 'relatively mild'.

At the time of the Korean War there were about 30 million people living there, nine million in the north, the rest south of the 38th Parallel. The north contained most of the natural resources, such as gold, wood, iron, copper and graphite and was quite industrialised and consequently much richer than the backward south. They even exported hydro-electric power to South Korea, whose population existed mainly on primitive agriculture. Since the end of the war South Korea has made a spectacular 'leap forward', thanks to generous help from the USA, but in 1950 most of the peasants lived in mud brick and wattle houses in small villages. Those in towns, especially the refugees from the north, lived in possibly even worse conditions. However, as the photographs in this section show, the people were a calm, dignified race of Mongol stock, with Mongol features. They possessed (and still possess) a natural grace and beauty, which

Left: A little Korean girl brings home a string of locusts to supplement her family diet. *UN*

Above: Orphan Island. Nearly 1,000 orphans from Seoul, were evacuated during the fighting and sheltered on Cheju Island in an orphanage run by United Nations Civil Assistance Command officers. *UN*

Right: A family in a village near Seoul are seen here at breakfast — their largest meal of the day. The meal starts with soup and includes rice, egg plant, radish, radish leaves and beans. In accordance with Korean custom, the men eat at separate tables from the women. *UN*

Above: In a village near Pusan an old woman lays out red peppers to dry in the sun. *UN*

Above right: Typical Korean elders. Old age is much revered in Korea. *UN*

Right: A farmer carries a load of hay on the widely used 'A' frame. *UN*

is particularly apparent among the young. To Western eyes they were, like the Japanese, apparently inured to suffering and privation, and because of this seemed brutal and callous. Although there is evidence that Korean guards in POW camps were probably the most brutal, it is unfair to condemn the whole race, indeed Chinese historians called Korea 'the land of scholars and gentlemen', having a 2,000-year old civilisation. One need only look at the children to see how delightful they are and how well they are generally treated. 'No matter how poor a family may be', wrote Robert T. Oliver, in his book *The Truth about Korea,* 'the first matter upon which parents pride themselves is to have their children well fed and well clothed. Visitors in the countryside have been repeatedly struck by the neatness of the children's dress, however hard the living conditions may be'. Respect for age, following the teachings of Confucius is very marked. When meeting a Korean who is clearly older than you are, it is considered polite to ask his age, then to bow slightly and say: *'sung sangnim'* (my elder one). The old men dressed in white, even when they were carrying firewood on an A-frame. Religion in Korea was closely related to ancestor worship, although the main orthodox faith of the country was Buddhism.

How it all began

On 2 September 1945 the Japanese forces in Korea surrendered, those above the 38th Parallel to the troops of the Soviet Union, and those below it to United States forces. This brought to an end Japanese control in the area which had first begun in 1910. Later in 1945, in December, the Moscow Agreement between the USA, USSR and UK provided for a Joint Commission to be set up 'with a view to the re-establishment of Korea as an independent state'. It consisted of representatives from the United States command in the south and the Russian command in the north, and was established to help in forming a provisional Korean government. After a suitable government had been formed, the Commission, in consultation with the government, was to prepare and present proposals for a four-power trusteeship of Korea, which was then due to last for a period of five years, to China, Russia, America and Great Britain. Unfortunately, the Joint Commission, which held its first meeting in March 1946, quickly reached an impasse. The problem was that Russia would not agree that all the Korean people should have a say in the formation of the provisional government, but said that it should be only those who had not objected to the trusteeship plan — there had been widespread objections voiced by a majority of Koreans about the trusteeship plan as they felt, with good reason, that it would merely delay their achievement of full sovereignty for yet another five years. The only ones not to object had been the Communists, who, under orders from the Kremlin, had remained deliberately silent. The USA refused to accept the Russian plan which would have denied the vast majority of the Korean people a say in establishing their own government. The impasse continued until the autumn of 1947, when the USA submitted the problem to the General Assembly of the United Nations. Despite the General Assembly adopting a resolution which created a United Nations Temporary Commission on Korea, no real progress was made and the eventual

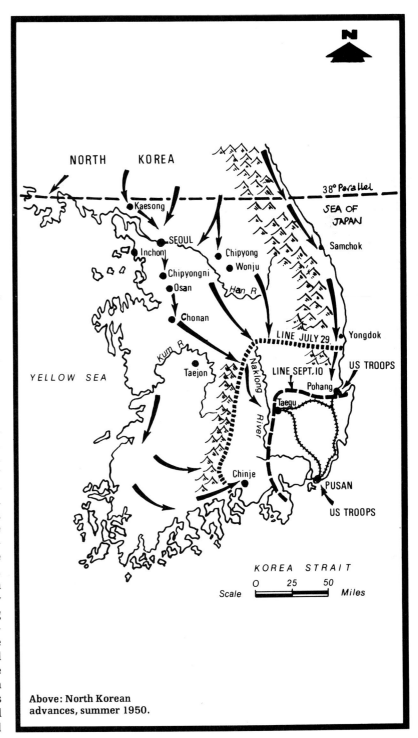

Above: North Korean advances, summer 1950.

outcome was a division of the country along the now famous 38th Parallel, with the Soviets installing their own puppet government in the *Democratic People's Republic of Korea* in the north, while the *Republic of Korea* in the south was recognised as the only government in the area by the rest of the world, and was allowed to apply for membership of the United Nations in early 1949. The Democratic People's Republic also applied, but was refused membership.

With aid, mainly from the United States, the South Koreans began to rebuild their warblighted country, hindered at every turn by those north of the 38th Parallel. This started with the cutting off of all electrical power to the south which the industrialised north had always previously provided. As the South Koreans struggled to improve their lot, the Soviets began training and equipping the North Korean Army, building up its strength with the intention of striking at South Korea when the time was ripe. That moment came at 4am on Sunday 25 June 1950, when thousands of North Korean troops poured across the frontier. Seven infantry divisions, supported by a brigade of T-34 tanks and strike aircraft, moved rapidly south, meeting little opposition from the four ill-equipped South Korean divisions stationed on the border. Clearly this was an all-out bid to dominate the entire peninsula under Communist control. Radio Pyongyang falsely asserted that the South Koreans had initiated the attack and that they had been forced to declare war and to mount a counter-attack against 'the aggressors'! The ROK Army, armed mainly with hand carried weapons, was no match for the well-equipped Communist divisions of General Chai Ung Chai, as they swept southwards along six invasion routes. Surprised and stunned the South Koreans turned desperately to the rest of the world for help. That very afternoon the UN Security Council had been holding an emergency meeting and declared the attack a 'breach of the peace', calling for an immediate end to hostilities and a withdrawal by the attackers. Two days later, when no notice had been taken by North Korea, the Council recommended that UN member states should furnish aid to South Korea in order to repel the attack and restore peace and security in the area. The resolution was supported by 53 UN member states, and of those 17 eventually sent troops to join the forces of the Republic of Korea in fighting off the invaders, while supplies, food and equipment were sent by 49 nations and scores of voluntary agencies. This was the first time in history that an assembly of governments, representing most of the peoples of the world, had met together and decided to help a small country which had been invaded, thus honouring the pledge of the nations under the UN Charter to 'unite our strength to maintain individual peace and security . . . and to ensure . . . that armed force shall not be used save in common interest.'

Below: Front page of *Pacific Stars and Stripes* at the start of the war.
Pacific Stars and Stripes

14

Brief description of the Korean War

The initial phase of the war in Korea, which began with the Communist invasion on 25 June 1950, saw first the weak South Korean forces, and then those of the United States Army which had been hastily sent over from Japan, having to give ground in front of the much more powerful, better equipped and more purposeful North Korean Army. Throughout July the retreat continued until the only territory that remained to the hard pressed UN forces was a small perimeter around the vital port of Pusan. Even this was being continually whittled away, as throughout August and early September the North Koreans mounted attack after attack to drive the UN forces into the sea. Fortunately the UN ground forces, which were by now known collectively as the Eighth United States Army — the very first army in history to be employed by the United Nations in the cause of world peace — were well supported by both air and sea. The North Korean air force was quickly destroyed almost completely, thus giving the UN forces complete command of the skies, while off the coasts the US Seventh Fleet soon controlled the sea flanks. Thanks to this support and to the additional UN forces which were now beginning to arrive — such as the British 27th Infantry Brigade from Hong Kong — Gen Walton H. Walker, commander of the Eighth Army, was not only able to hold all the enemy assaults, but also to prepare a counter-attack. The master stroke in the UN plan was undoubtedly the boldly conceived and brilliantly executed landings by US X Corps under Gen Edward M. Almond at Inchon at dawn on 15 September 1950, which led directly to the recapture of the South Korean capital of Seoul. The landings were the 'brain-child' of the Supreme Commander of all UN Forces in Korea, the world' famous American Gen Douglas MacArthur. In coordination with the landings, the Eighth Army launched an all-out offensive on 16 September, breaking out of the Pusan perimeter and rapidly driving the enemy out of Korea.

The United Nations was soon faced with the difficult decision as to whether or not they should authorise their forces to cross the 38th Parallel, so that they could follow up and destroy the North Korean Army. This was eventually passed by the General Assembly, despite grave warnings that the Chinese would take action if the American troops entered North Korea. The victorious UN forces pressed on, capturing Pyongyang, capital of North Korea, on 19 October. The following day X Corps struck again from the sea, this time carrying out an unopposed landing at Wonsan on the east coast. Five days later, the first South Korean troops reached the Yalu River at Chosan. Gen MacArthur, full of confidence and convinced that the Chinese were bluffing, ordered a general advance to the Yalu, telling the troops that they would be 'Home for Christmas'.

Unfortunately he could not have been more wrong. On the night of the 25 November, 180,000 Chinese troops launched a massive offensive against the right flank of the Eighth Army, pouring through a gap between it and the X Corps. The more lightly equipped Chinese troops were ideally situated to the rugged Korean terrain and quickly nullified the superior firepower of their road-bound opponents, forcing them into a costly, headlong withdrawal. In bitterly cold weather, destroying vast dumps of stores on the way, the entire Eighth Army was forced to retreat; while X Corps just managed to extricate itself by sea from Hungnam, north of their landing side at Wonsan. Suffering heavy casualties, the UN forces fell back in front of the massive Chinese onslaught. Gen Walker managed to stabilise the situation on the 38th Parallel in the last week of December, but this was only a brief respite. On 1 January 1951, the enemy launched another all-out attack over the 38th Parallel and captured Seoul for a second time a few days later. Sadly Gen Walker was killed in mid-January in a jeep accident, his place being taken by another famous American soldier, Gen Matthew B. Ridgway. The Eighth Army

Above: General of the Armies Douglas McArthur makes a pre-invasion inspection of the landing areas in Inchon harbour, aboard Admiral Struble's launch, 15 September 1950. *US Army*

Far right, top: Lt-Gen Matthew Bunker Ridgway, CG Eighth Army confers with Brig-Gen Van Brut somewhere near the front. It is easy to see why Gen Ridgway was known by his troops, somewhat irreverently, as 'Old Iron Tits'! *UN (from US Army)*

Far right, bottom: View of a public meeting held in a school-house at Masan in August 1950, by the United Nations Commission on Korea. *UN (from US Army)*

attempted to hold the enemy behind the Han River, but soon had to fall back.

However, by mid-January it was clear that the enemy was running out of steam and Gen Ridgway was able to go on to the offensive and to conduct strong armed reconnaissance and local counter-attacks to win back key positions. Seoul was recaptured on 14 March as a result of Operation 'Ripper', launched a week earlier. During the second half of March, the strength of the enemy resistance at last began to weaken and they started a general withdrawal. By 8 April, all Chinese and North Korean troops had withdrawn from South Korea and the front was again roughly stabilised along the 38th Parallel. There followed a short period of stability on the battlefront while events were completely overshadowed by the relief of Gen MacArthur by President Truman. Truman was forced into this situation by MacArthur's insistence that the battle should be carried into Chinese territory, using all weapons at his disposal, even nuclear if necessary, to deal with the Communist 'sanctuary' north of the Yalu River. While MacArthur felt that everything should be done to defeat the enemy, Truman and the American Government could see themselves being forced into another world war, with Russia invading Western Europe, while the USA was involved fighting the Chinese. Truman showed considerable firmness and resolve in dealing with a man who was at the time

considered by many to be America's greatest living soldier, a man who was treated almost like a god in some areas. In the end he prevailed, MacArthur was sacked and the war confined to Korea. ('... MacArthur left me no choice,' declared Truman, 'I could no longer tolerate his insubordination.') Gen Ridgway took over from MacArthur as Supreme Commander, and Lt-Gen James A. Van Fleet, was appointed to command the Eighth Army.

The Chinese attacked again on the night of 22 April. By the end of the month they had been contained at the cost of large numbers of casualties to both sides — the Chinese alone losing an estimated 70,000 men, while there were many epic feats of courage among the UN troops, such as the famous stand of the Gloucesters at the Imjin River. The second phase of the Chinese offensive opened on 15 May, the main weight being on the east side of the peninsula. Again there was bitter fighting as the UN troops strove to hold off repeated Chinese attacks. This time, however, the enemy soon ran out of steam, and the UN were able to go on to the offensive themselves, and to force the Reds back across the now well trodden 38th Parallel. During early June the Communists had to concentrate all their efforts on delaying the advance of the Eighth Army, but by the 15th the UN troops had reached almost all their planned objectives and had begun to establish another defensive line some dis-

tance north of the Parallel — 15 to 20 miles in the west and centre and up to 35 miles in the east.

While the new defensive line was being established, enemy action was restricted to minor probing operations only: indeed UN patrols were able to penetrate as far as 10 miles forward without meeting proper enemy resistance. Clearly the Communists had suffered a heavy defeat and it would take them some time to recover. However, it was estimated that there were still more than 70 enemy divisions in North Korea, so the UN Command could not afford to relax its vigilance. This became increasingly important as the Reds began to hint that they might be prepared to consider opening peace talks to end the conflict, while the USA let it be known that they would be prepared to accept a permanent division of the peninsula at the 38th Parallel. Statements were made by the Soviet representative at the United Nations, Jacob Malik, who, in a radio broadcast on 22 April sponsored by the UN, said that they might be prepared to discuss a ceasefire in Korea. Immediately everyone

began to imagine that peace was only a matter of a few weeks away. Gen Ridgway was instructed to invite the Communists to discuss the possibility of a ceasefire. On 30 June 1951, he sent the following message to his opposite number, the C-in-C, Communist Forces in Korea: 'I am informed that you may wish a meeting to discuss an armistice, providing a cessation of hostilities and all acts of armed force in Korea, with adequate guarantees for the maintenance of such an armistice. Upon receipt of word from you that such a meeting is desired, I shall be prepared to name my representatives. I propose that such a meeting could take place aboard a Danish hospital ship in Wonsan harbour.' Peking replied the following day: 'We have received your statement dated 30 June 1951, concerning peace negotiations. Having been empowered to do so, we hereby declare that we agree to meet your representatives to negotiate peace in order to cease hostilities and restore peace. If you agree, our representatives will make preparations to meet your representatives between 10 and 15 July 1951.' The reply

was signed by General Kim T. Sung, C-in-C of the Korean People's Army and Gen Peng Te-Huai, C-in-C of the Chinese People's Volunteer Forces. The first meeting took place on 8 July 1951.

The high hopes of the UN representatives that the ceasefire would be quickly achieved were soon dashed. Clearly the Communists were prepared to make the whole procedure a long drawn out affair, enabling them to extract as much propaganda value and other advantages as they could dream up. It would of course do them no good to agree to an immediate ceasefire while they were still at the disadvantage of having just suffered a resounding defeat. At the same time they realised that the Eighth Army would be accused of jeopardising any chances of peace if they were to take advantage of the battlefield situation and continue their pressure. The Communists were thus 'off the hook' and could conduct the 'peace negotiations' at their leisure, while they built up their strength again on the battlefield.

It is hardly surprising, therefore, to dis-

cover that the peace talks dragged on and on for a further two years, the final armistice not being signed until 27 July, 1953. On the battlefield, the war of movement had ended. Neither side ever again launched a full-scale offensive, nor did they risk large numbers of casualties in a major bid for total victory. But the fighting went on. In conditions which resembled those in the trenches of World War 1, men fought and died in local attacks, patrolling, artillery bombardments and so on. As Brig-Gen S. L. A. Marshall, Operations Analyst of the Eighth Army in Korea, put it in his excellent short history of the war entitled *The Military History of the Korean War*: 'Local attacks were mounted by both sides to keep troops from going stale and to demonstrate a readiness for resumption of unlimited fighting. These exercises took a heavy toll of life without really helping either side. Both the Communists and the UN built their power higher, the former increasing troop strength, the latter augmenting its weapons and adding more artillery and tank units.' Military initiative had become subordinated to the truce negotiations, but the battling, although now more muted, still went on and the casualty figures on both sides mounted. The major difference between the two lines of battlefield fortifications was brought about by the lack of air power on the Communist side and their much larger availability of manpower. The Chinese became so expert at the art of camouflage that there were never any easily identifiable gun positions, command posts or other tell-tale features. Deep underground shelters, impervious to the UN air bombing and heavy artillery, were constructed on the reverse slopes of the Communist-held hills, while on the UN side smaller numbers of troops depended upon masses of barbed wire, minefields, heavily sandbagged and more obvious earthworks, to gain their protection.

At Kaesong, just inside Communist lines, the peace talks began and then broke down. After further UN attacks, the Communists asked for them to be reopened, this time at Panmunjon which became the permanent site for the talks. On and on dragged the arguments at the new location for a period of about 18 months, broken only when one team or the other withdrew for a temporary period. At the front the troops had to face a second bitter winter, but by April 1953, the news was a little brighter. The Communists had agreed to exchange all sick and wounded prisoners of war, and by June even the emotive issue of what should happen to POWs who said that they did not want to return to their own country had been resolved. Unfortunately, it was now the turn of South Korea to hold up proceedings. President Rhee declared that he would not agree to any armistice which left Korea divided and subsequently arranged for the escape of some 25,000 North Korean anti-communist POWs from their camps. This dramatic action led to renewed fighting, as the Chinese launched a determined offensive in the eastern and central sectors of the front. The fighting continued for over a month, almost right up to the day of the signing of the ceasefire agreement. Undoubtedly this final offensive was designed to make the South Koreans agree to the armistice terms, rather than to break the UN line, although it did achieve deep penetrations in some places. At least 50,000 Chinese troops were involved and heavy casualties resulted on both sides.

Three years, one month and two days after the original unprovoked invasion of South Korea, the armistice agreement was at long last signed, at 10.00 hours on the morning of 27 July 1953. Lt-Gen William Harrison and Gen Nam II signed the 18 copies of the agreement at Panmunjon, while Gen Mark W. Clark, as Commander in Chief, United Nations Command, countersigned the agreement that afternoon at Munsan. The representative of the Republic of Korea did not attend. The armistice covered the following points:

a   The Demarcation Line was defined and ran approximately along the front lines of the opposing armies. Both sides were to withdraw two kilometres from the Demarcation Line so as to establish a Demilitarised Zone.

b   Hostilities were to cease 12 hours after the signing of the armistice. Within 72 hours all troops were to be out of the Demilitarised Zone. Neither side was to reinforce its troops, but normal rotation of reliefs was permitted. Both sides were to help and protect the various Commissions and Inspections Teams set up by the Agreement.

c   All POWs who wished to be repatriated were to be handed over within 60 days.

d   The military commanders on both sides recommended to their governments that a political conference be set up within 90 days to draw up a Korean Peace Treaty.

Two weeks later, the UN nations who had fought in Korea, published the following joint statement: 'We affirm, in the interest of world peace, that if there is a renewal of armed attacks, challenging again the principles of the United Nations, we should again be united and prompt to resist. The consequences of such a breach of the armistice would be so grave that, in all probability, it would not be possible to confine hostilities within the frontiers of Korea.' So ended the Korean War. It was no tremendous victory, but at least it could be said that the United Nations had triumphed over Communism and saved the Republic of Korea. It temporarily halted the spread of Communism in the Far East and prevented World War III, and yet is probably the least known about war of modern times.

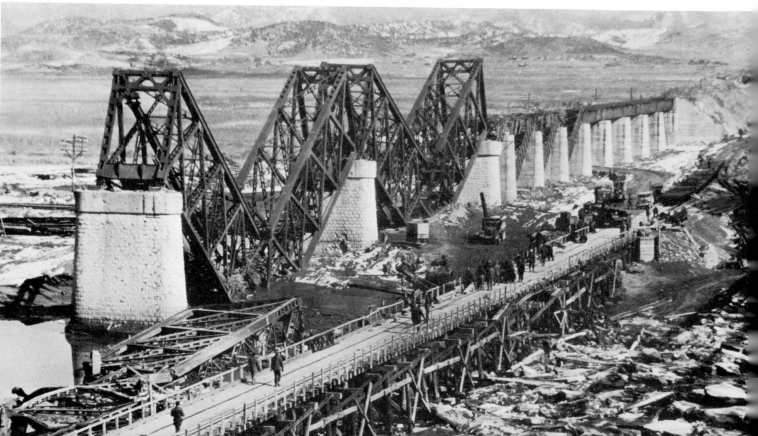

Below: Freedom Gate Bridge spanning the Imjin River was built by the 84th Engineer Construction Battalion, US Eighth Army, 10 March 1952. *US Army*

The opposing armies

North and South Korea

At the start of the war, the North Korean Army was far superior to that of the South, so a quick conquest was inevitable. During the first half of 1950, the Korean People's Army had doubled in size to nearly 200,000 troops, divided into 10 infantry divisions and supporting units, organised along Russian lines and equipped with mainly Russian-made weapons. Most importantly, they had the weapons for a successful 'Blitzkrieg' — 240 of one of the best tanks of World War 2, the T-34/85 which mounted a hard hitting 85mm gun, and over 200 Yak fighters. Without these two weapons there could have been no aggression. The ROK Army totalled 98,000 and like the 45,000 strong National Police, it was armed chiefly with hand carried weapons, such as rifles and carbines. Its eight infantry divisions were 'paper tigers', incapable of moving quickly or of stopping an armoured assault. It is small wonder then that by the end of June, only five days into the war, the North Koreans were in possession of all the territory north of the Han River and had shattered most of the ROK forces. Almost half of the army — about 44,000 troops — had been killed, captured or were missing. Only two ROK divisions, the 6th and the 8th were able to retreat with their weapons and equipment intact. Many of the 54,000 troops that were left to defend their shattered country had lost even their personal weapons and equipment. It took a lot of determination and hard work to rebuild the ROK into an efficient and well trained fighting force, capable of protecting their homeland, but this was achieved during the last two years of the war. A major contribution was made in this achievement by the men of the US Military Advisory Group to the Republic of Korea, or 'KMAG' as it was normally called.

First to answer the plea for assistance from South Korea was the US Seventh Fleet and the Japan-based US Fifth Air Force. It was hoped that the threat of using US ground forces would be sufficient to deter the North Koreans and make them withdraw. Even if US ground troops had to

Below: A line-up of United Nations troops (l to r): America, Belgium, Greece, Korea, Luxembourg, Puerto Rico and the Virgin Islands. *US Army*

Above: The British Soldier.
Private Bill Speakman, VC.
Speakman of the Black Watch
was attached to 1 KOSB and
won his VC for heroism on
4 November 1951. *IWM*

Above right: Men of the French
battalion on patrol.
ECP Armees

Right: Australian soldier, 1953
model, wears a nylon 'flak'
vest, carries a Sterling
submachine gun and a beltfull
of Mills 36 grenades.
Australian War Memorial

land, then they would — they were told — merely be used in what was optimistically termed as a 'police action'. When it became clear that this threat had failed, two infantry divisions, initially the 24th, followed by the 25th, were sent to Korea from Japan by air and sea. As we shall see from the first battle account, these US soldiers completely underestimated their opponents. They did not realise that their weapons were inferior, their soldiers 'green' and soft, and showed it the first time they had to face enemy fire. Despite a great deal of individual acts of bravery, and none was braver than the divisional commander of 24 Division, Maj-Gen William F. Dean who won the Congressional Medal of Honor before being captured, they were badly mauled by the North Koreans.

The UN Army

The soldiers of 15 nations came to the assistance of South Korea — see the nearby table for details. A further five provided medical assistance to the ground troops. As one reporter put it: 'They came from the four corners of the world — from

Above: Maj-Gen William M. Hoge, Commander IX Corps, decorates one of the Greek battalion, April 1951. *UN*

Ground units provided by the United Nations		
Country	*Major formation(s)*	*Date first arrived*
USA	seven infantry divisions, one marine division, logistical and support forces	2 July 1950
Australia	two infantry battalions	28 September 1950
Canada	one infantry brigade, one field artillery regiment, one armoured regiment and units	7 November 1950
New Zealand	one field artillery regiment and support units	31 December 1950
United Kingdom	two composite infantry brigades with supporting units	28 August 1950
Belgium	one infantry battalion	31 January 1951
Colombia	one infantry battalion	15 June 1951
Ethiopia	one infantry battalion	7 May 1951
France	one infantry battalion	29 November 1951
Greece	one infantry battalion	9 December 1950
Netherlands	one infantry battalion	23 November 1950
Philippines	one infantry battalion	19 September 1950
Thailand	one infantry battalion	7 November 1950
Turkey	one infantry brigade	17 October 1950
Luxembourg	one infantry platoon	31 January 1951
Denmark	medical team (also a hospital ship)	7 March 1951
India	one field ambulance (served with 1st Commonwealth Division)	20 November 1950 20 November 1950
Italy	one Red Cross hospital	16 November 1951
Norway	one mobile surgical hospital	22 June 1951
Sweden	one field hospital	28 September 1950

America, Europe, Africa, Asia and the Antipodes. There were tall dark, fierce men from Ethiopia, laughing little Siamese, swarthy Latins, fair Texans, men that sang and dour men.' They were all very different. Those from the smaller countries of the world often fought outstandingly well, as though they felt that their prestige was at stake, not just in the face of the enemy, but rather in the eyes of their bigger allies. For a large part of the war (from July 1951) the Commonwealth troops were grouped together into one unique division in which every single one of them had a fierce pride. Other countries, such as Turkey, produced a complete brigade of fearsome fighting men, while the backbone of the UN Army undoubtedly came from the eight US divisions and all their logistical and administrative backup units — containing far more troops than all the rest put together. 'If this unique war proved anything about soldiers,' concluded an article on the UN forces by Stephen Barber in the *Egyptian Mail* of 1 August 1953, 'it proved that such an alliance is working in the field no matter what squabbling may go on between politicians ... It proved that where leadership counts is at squad, company and battalion level ... The sense of comradeship in arms is more important than propaganda, psychiatrists, entertainers, comforts and the like. The common danger and common discomfort, rather than a deep sense of common cause, bound this UN Army together. Its commanders could rely on it'.

24

Left: A US Marine sergeant (in helmet) helps train Korean police for rear area guard duties. *US Marine Corps*

Below left: M/Sgt Chang Kyung Shik of the ROK Army, lost his leg in the battle of Ongjin peninsula at the beginning of the war. *UN*

Right: 'KATCOM' soldiers attached to the 3rd Royal 22e Regiment, are briefed for a reconnaissance patrol. *Public Archives Canada*

Below: A group of North Korean prisoners. *UN*

Right: Li Ching-yuan of the Chinese People's Volunteers, studies orders on the treatment of war prisoners.
Chinese People's Committee for World Peace

Below: Canadians look over dispirited Chinese prisoners taken by 25th Brigade during the advance to the 38th Parallel in May 1951.
Public Archives Canada

The Chinese forces

The elements of the Chinese People's Liberation Army (PLA) which entered Korea did so in the autumn of 1950, when the UN appeared to be within an ace of victory over the North Koreans. From then on they took a major part in the war and became the principal enemy of the UN forces. By the end of 1952, it was estimated that the strength of the Chinese Communist Forces in Korea (CCF) had risen to over a million men, supported by at least 500 tanks and 1,000 jet aircraft. I will leave describing their ground forces until later, but undoubtedly they were brave, tough and excellent soldiers, who followed a simple tactical doctrine which was expressed thus: 'If the enemy attacks we defend. If his attack is too strong we withdraw. When he is tired, we attack. When he withdraws, we pursue and kill.'

Withdrawal action

This first story is not a pleasant one. There is no great and glorious victory at the end of it, nor indeed does much go right for the 'Good Guys' from start to finish. It is a sad saga of overconfident, unfit, green troops, who were soft after months of living 'high on the hog' in the fleshpots of Japan, receiving a bloody lesson in basic soldiering from an enemy for whom they had nothing but contempt. But it has to be told, because it sets the scene for a war in which many of the United Nations soldiers who took part had to learn the hard way about the simple things of war, such as looking after their equipment, their weapons and themselves, of keeping their personal arms clean and serviceable, of teamwork, of obeying orders and of leadership. In other words, all those basic essentials which go towards making a good soldier and an efficient fighting unit, that we are all too often inclined to take for granted. Above all it shows that cockiness is no substitute for high morale, and how quickly panic can spread in a badly led, demoralised force, which is kept in total ignorance of the true battle situation. The story comes from an excellent book entitled *Combat Actions in Korea*, produced by the Office of the Chief of Military History of the United States Army, and quoted here with their kind permission. Before criticising the men of the 24th US Infantry Division who feature in this story, we should perhaps offer up a silent prayer, remembering situations in which we too were not up to scratch and maybe say with feeling, 'there but for the grace of God go I'. The faults stick out like sore thumbs. However, the main question which must be asked is, did these troops learn by their mistakes? I believe that they did, and the proof is that the final shaky perimeter around the one remaining port of Pusan was held, and the enemy was eventually turned back. As the US Army military historian commented in his summing up of the debacle: 'It was to take many months of combat and physical hardening before the military proficiency of both officers and men was realised and they achieved the high military proficiency of which they were capable.'

'Korean summers are wet. It was raining and unseasonably cold during the dark, early morning hours of 5 July 1950, when 1st Battalion, 34th Infantry reached Pyongtaek. Approximately 40 miles south of Seoul, the village was near the west coast of Korea on the main road and railroad between the capital city and Taejon, Taegu, and Pusan to the south. Pyongtaek was a shabby huddle of colourless huts, lining narrow, dirty streets. The infantrymen stood quietly in the steady rain, waiting for daylight. They grumbled about the weather but, in the sudden shift from garrison duties in Japan, few appeared to be concerned about the possibility of combat in Korea. None expected to stay there long. High-ranking officers and riflemen alike shared the belief that a few American soldiers would restore order within a few weeks. "As soon as those North Koreans see an American uniform over here," the soldiers boasted to one another, "they'll run like hell." American soldiers later lost this cocky attitude when the North Koreans overran their first defensive position. Early overconfidence changed to surprise, then to dismay, and finally to the grim realisation that, of the two armies, the North Korean force was superior in size, equipment, training and fighting ability. As part of the 24th Infantry Division, the 1st Battalion, 34th Infantry was one of several unprepared American battalions rushed from Japan to help halt the North Korean invasion of the southern end of the Korean peninsula. The change from garrison to combat duties had come abruptly on the morning of 1 July 1950, when the division commander (Maj-Gen William F. Dean) called the commander of the 34th Infantry and alerted the entire regiment for immediate movement to Korea. At the time the regiment consisted of only two understrength battalions. 24 hours later they sailed from Sasebo, Kyushu, arriving in

Pusan that evening. After spending two days checking equipment, organising supplies, and arranging for transportation north, the regiment, crowded into five South Korean-operated trains, had started north on the afternoon of 4 July.

'The 34th Infantry had not been the first unit of the United States Army to reach Korea. Part of the 1st Battalion, 21st Infantry (24th Division) had been airlifted from Japan on the morning of 1 July. After landing at Pusan it had boarded trains immediately and rushed northwards. The battalion commander (Lt-Col Charles B. Smith) had the mission of setting up roadblocks to halt the North Korean southward thrust. Part of his force had gone to Pyongtaek and part to Ansong, a village ten miles east of Pyongtaek.

'Without making contact with the North Koreans, the two task forces from Col Smith's battalion had reached their assigned areas during the morning of 3 July. A field artillery battery arrived at Pyongtaek the next day, and that evening, 4 July, Smith's entire force had moved 12 miles north of Pyongtaek where it set up another blocking position just north of Osan. About the same time that Smith's battalion had started for Osan, the two battalions of the 34th Infantry, heading north, had passed through Taejon. One battalion was to re-establish the blocking position at Ansong; the 1st Battalion was going to Pyongtaek with a similar mission. A new commander — an experienced combat officer — had joined the 1st Battalion as the trains moved through Taejon. He told his company commanders that the North Korean soldiers were reported to be farther north but that they were poorly trained, that only half of them had weapons, and that there would be no difficulty in stopping them. Junior Officers had assured their men that after a brief police action all would be back in Sasebo. Officers of the 34th Infantry knew that the 21st was ahead of the 34th in a screening position. Overconfidence was the prevailing note.

'This was the background and setting for the rainy morning when the 1st Battalion — and especially Company A, with which this account is mainly concerned — waited in the muddy streets of Pyongtaek. When daylight came, the companies marched north to the hills upon which they were to set up their blocking position. A small river flowed along the north side of Pyongtaek. Two miles north of the bridge that carried the main highway across the river there were two grassy-covered hills separated by a strip of rice paddies three-quarters of a mile wide. The railroad and

narrow dirt road, both on 8-10ft high embankments, ran through the neatly patterned fields. The battalion commanders stationed Company B on the east side of the road, Company A on the west, leaving Company C in reserve positions in the rear. Once on the hill, the men dropped their packs and began digging into the coarse red earth to prepare defensive positions for an enemy attack few of them expected. In Company A's sector the positions consisted of two-man foxholes dug across the north side of the hill, across the rice paddies and the railroad embankment, and beyond that to the road. Company A (Capt Leroy Osburn) consisted of about 140 men and officers at the time. With two men in each position, the holes were so far apart that the men had to shout to one another. Each man was equipped with either an M1 rifle or a carbine for which he carried between 80 and 100 rounds of ammunition. The Weapons Platoon had three 60mm mortars. There were also three light machine guns — one in each of the rifle platoons — and four boxes of ammunition for each machine gun. Each platoon had one BAR (Browning Automatic Rifle) and 200 rounds of ammunition for it. There were no grenades, nor was there any ammunition for the recoilless rifles.

'To the north of Osan, meanwhile, Col Smith's 1st Battalion, 21st Infantry and an attached battery of artillery completed the occupation of the high ground north of the village by daylight on 5 July. Smith had orders to hold in place to gain time, even

Above: One of the very few field artillery pieces of the ROK Army, firing in support of the 1st Korean Infantry Division as they desperately try to hold back the North Korean invasion, July 1950.
US Army from UN

Above right: American troops with a 105mm howitzer towed by a 2½ton truck, move up to the front lines in an early dawn move.
UN (from US Army)

Right: The first American tank to fight in Korea was *Rebel's Roost*, an M24 Chaffee, seen here after returning from the front as the crew clean and service their weapons.
US Army via Patton Museum

though his forces might become surrounded. That same morning, at 0745, enemy tanks approached from the north. The Americans opened fire with artillery and then with bazookas, but the tanks rammed through the infantry positions and on south past the artillery, after losing only four of 33 tanks. Enemy infantrymen followed up later, engaged Col Smith's force and, after a four-hour battle, almost surrounded it. About 1400, Col Smith ordered his men to leave the position and withdraw toward Ansong. Smith's force carried out as many wounded as possible, but abandoned its equipment and dead. The survivors, travelling on foot in small groups or on the few artillery trucks, headed south-west toward Ansong. This was the result of the first engagement between North Korean and American soldiers. Brig-Gen George B. Barth (commander of 24th Division Artillery and Gen Dean's representative in the forward area) was at Osan with the battery of artillery when the first "Fire Mission!" was relayed to the battery position. When it became

apparent that neither the infantry nor the artillery could stop the tanks, Gen Barth had gone back to Pyongtaek to alert the 1st Battalion, 34th Infantry, which was still digging in. The 1st Battalion's command post was in one of the dirty buildings on the road north of Pyongtaek. It was apparent to Gen Barth, by the time he arrived there, that enemy tanks would break through the Osan position. He therefore warned the 1st Battalion commander and instructed him to dispatch a patrol northward to make contact with the enemy column. Barth's instructions to the 1st Battalion, 34th Infantry, differed from those he had given to Col Smith at Osan. Since Gen Barth now believed the Pyongtaek force could only hold out a short time if encircled, as apparently was happening to the battalion at Osan, he ordered the battalion at Pyongtaek to hold only until the enemy threatened to envelop the position, and then delay in successive rearward positions to gain time.

'A rifle platoon of the 34th Infantry went north to make contact with the enemy tanks. About halfway between Pyongtaek and Osan the platoon met several enemy tanks and fired upon them without effect. The tanks made no effort to advance. The opposing forces settled down to observing each other. While these events were taking place only a few miles away, men of Company A at Pyongtaek finished digging their defensive positions or sat quietly in the cold rain. In spite of the fact that a column of tanks had overrun the Osan position and was then not more than six miles from Pyongtaek, the infantrymen did not know about it. They continued to exchange rumours and speculation. One of the platoon leaders called his men together later that afternoon to put an end to the growing anxiety over the possibility of combat. ''You've been told repeatedly,'' he explained, ''that this is a police action, and that is exactly what it is going to be.'' He assured them that the rumours of a large enemy force in the area were false, and that they would be back in Sasebo within a few weeks. Later that evening however, Capt Osburn told some of the men that four Americans who had driven north of Osan toward Suwon had failed to return, and that he had heard an estimate that 12,000 North Koreans were in the area to the north. He considered an attack possible but not probable.

'It rained steadily all night. Beyond the fact that tanks had penetrated the Osan position, no more information about the fight came through until nearly midnight, when five survivors of Osan arrived at the 1st Battalion command post with a detailed account of that action. The 1st Battalion commander passed word of the Osan defeat along to his company commanders, warning them to be on the lookout for stragglers from the 21st Infantry. Apparently no one passed the information on down to the platoons. The battalion commander then sent a patrol from Company C to blow up a small bridge about 600 yards north of his two forward companies. It was about 0300 when this was done. Startled by the explosions, infantrymen of Company A showed concern until they learned the cause. Then they settled back to wait for daylight, or to sleep if possible. At 0430 they began to stir again. SFC Roy E. Collins, a platoon sergeant, walked along the row of foxholes in the centre of the company position. One of a group of combat-experienced men recently transferred from another division, he had joined Company A only the day before. He advised his men to get up and break out their C rations and eat while they had a chance. The evening before, Collins had stationed a two-man listening post in the rice paddies about 75yds north of the company. He called down and told them to come back to the company perimeter. It was only a few minutes after daylight. The battalion commander walked down the road between Companies A and B, stopping to talk to a group of 17 men manning a roadblock on Company A's side of the road. Lt Herman L. Driskell was in charge of the group, which consisted of an eight-man machine gun squad from his 1st Platoon and three 2.36in bazooka teams from the Weapons Platoon. After telling Driskell to get his men down into their holes because he planned to register the 4.2in mortars, the battalion commander walked across the soggy rice paddies toward Company A's command post on the top of the hill. Lt Driskell's men did not, however, get into their holes — the holes were full of water. A Weapons Platoon sergeant, SFC Jack C. Williams, and PFC James O. Hite, were sitting near one hole. ''I sure would hate to have to get into that hole,'' Hite said. In a few minutes they heard mortar shells overhead, but the shell bursts were lost in the morning fog and rain. In the cold rain, hunched under their ponchos, the men sat beside their holes eating their breakfast ration.

'Up on the hill, Sgt Collins was eating a can of beans. He had eaten about half of it when he heard the sound of engines running. Through the fog he saw the faint outline of several tanks that had stopped just beyond the bridge that the detail from Company C destroyed two hours earlier. North Korean soldiers from the lead tank

Top right: A US M26 tank crew 'bomb-up' in readiness for the North Korean assault, 21 August 1950.
US Army via Patton Museum

Bottom right: M26 tanks of the 73rd Heavy Tank Battalion move into position somewhere in Korea, 27 August 1950.
US Army via Patton Museum

Above: An M26 detours around a broken bridge in the Tabu-dong area, 24 August 1950.
US Army via Patton Museum

got out and walked up to inspect the bridge site. At the same time, through binoculars, Collins could see two columns of infantrymen moving beyond the tanks, around both ends of the bridge and out across the rice paddies. He yelled back to his platoon leader (Lt Robert R. Ridley), "Sir, we got company." Lt Ridley, having been warned that part of the 21st Infantry might be withdrawing down this road, said it was probably part of that unit. "Well," said Collins, "these people have tanks and I know that the 21st hasn't any." The battalion commander arrived at Capt Osburn's CP just in time to see the column of enemy infantrymen appear. Deciding that it was made up of men from the 21st Infantry, the two commanders watched it for several minutes before realising it was too large to be friendly troops. They could see a battalion-sized group already, and others were still coming in a column of fours. At once the battalion commander called for mortar fire. When the first round landed, the enemy spread out across the rice paddies on both sides of the road but continued to advance. By this time Collins could count 13 tanks from the blown bridge north to the point where the column disappeared in the early morning fog. Within a few minutes the men from the enemy's lead tank returned to their vehicle, got in, closed the turret and then swung the tube until it pointed directly toward Company A. "Get down!" Sgt Collins yelled to his men. "Here it comes!" The first shell exploded just above the row of foxholes spattering dirt over the centre platoon. The men slid into their holes. Collins and two other combat veterans of

World War 2 began shouting to their men to commence firing. Response was slow although the Americans could see the North Korean infantrymen advancing steadily, spreading out across the flat ground in front of the hill. In the same hole with Sgt Collins were two riflemen. He poked them. "Come on," he said. "You've got an M1. Get firing."

'After watching the enemy attack for a few minutes, the battalion commander told Capt Osburn to withdraw Company A, and then left the hill, walking back to his command post, which he planned to move south. Out in front of the company hill, the two men at the listening post, after gathering up their wet equipment, had just been ready to leave when the first enemy shell landed. They jumped back into their hole. After a short time one of them jumped out and ran back under fire. The other, who stayed there, was never seen again. The entire 1st Platoon was also in the flat rice paddies. Lt Driskell's 17 men from 1st and the Weapons Platoon who were between the railroad and the road could hear some of the activity, but they could not see the enemy because of the high embankments on both sides. Pvt Hite was still sitting by his water-filled hole when the first enemy shell exploded up on the hill. He thought a 4.2in mortar shell had fallen short. Within a minute or two another round landed near Osburn's CP on top of the hill. Pvt Hite watched as the smoke drifted away. "Must be another short round," he remarked to Sgt Williams. "It's not short," said Williams, a combat-experienced soldier, "It's an enemy shell." Hite slid into his foxhole, making a dull splash like a frog diving into a pond. Williams followed. The two men sat there, up to their necks in cold, stagnant water.

'It was fully 15 minutes before the two Company A platoons up on the hill had built up an appreciable volume of fire, and less than half of the men were firing their weapons. The squad and platoon leaders did most of the firing. Many of the riflemen appeared stunned and unwilling to believe that enemy soldiers were firing at them. About 50 rounds fell in the battalion area within 15 minutes following the first shell-burst in Company A's sector. Meanwhile, enemy troops were appearing in numbers that looked overwhelmingly large to the American soldiers. "It looked like the entire city of New York moving against two little under-strength companies," said one of the men. Another large group of North Korean soldiers gathered around the tanks now lined up bumper to bumper on the road. It was the best target Sgt Collins had ever seen. He fretted because he had no

Above: Refugees trying to get away from Inchon during the North Korean offensive June 1950. *ROK Embassy, London*

ammunition for the recoiless rifle. Neither could he get mortar fire because the second enemy tank's shell had exploded near the 4.2in mortar observer who, although not wounded, had suffered severely from shock. In the confusion no one else attempted to direct the mortars. Within 30 minutes after the action began, the leading North Korean foot soldiers had moved so close that Company A men could see them load and reload their rifles. About the same time, Company B, under the same attack, began moving off the hill on the opposite side of the road. Within another minute or two Capt Osburn called down to tell his men to prepare to withdraw, "but we'll have to cover Baker Company first." Company A, however had no effective fire power and spent no time covering the movement of the other company. Most of the Weapons Platoon, located on the south side of the hill, left immediately, walking down to a cluster of about 15 straw-topped houses at the south edge of the hill. The two rifle platoons on the hill began to move out soon after Capt Osburn gave the alert order. The movement was orderly at the beginning although few of the men carried their field packs with them and others walked away leaving ammunition — even their weapons. However, just as the last two squads of this group reached a small ridge on the east side of the main hill, an enemy machine gun suddenly fired into the group. The men took off in panic. Capt Osburn and several of his platoon leaders were near the cluster of houses behind the hill re-forming the company for the march back to Pyongtaek. But when the panicked men raced past them, fear spread quickly

and others also began running. The officers called to them but few of the men stopped. Gathering as many members of his company as he could, Osburn sent them back towards the village with one of his officers.

'By this time the Weapons Platoon and most of the 2nd and 3rd Platoons had succeeded in vacating their positions. As they left, members of these units had called down telling the 1st Platoon to withdraw from its position blocking the road. Strung out across the flat paddies, the 1st Platoon was more exposed to enemy fire. Four of its men started running back and one, hit by rifle fire, fell. After seeing that, most of the others were apparently too frightened to leave their holes. As it happened, Lt Driskell's 17 men who were between the railroad and road embankments were unable to see the rest of the company. Since they had not heard the shouted order they were unaware that an order to withdraw had been given. They had, however, watched the fire fight between the North Koreans and Company B, and seen Company B leave. Lt Driskell and Sgt Williams decided that they would hold their ground until they received orders. Twenty or thirty minutes passed. As soon as the bulk of the two companies had withdrawn, the enemy fire stopped, and all became quiet again. Driskell and his 17 men were still in place when the North Koreans climbed the hill to take over the positions vacated by Company B. This roused their anxiety. "What do you think we should do now?" Driskell asked. "Well sir," said Sgt Williams, "I don't know what you are going to do, but I'd like to get the hell out of here." Driskell then sent a runner to see if the rest of the company was still in position. When the runner returned to say that he could see no one on the hill, the men started back using the railroad embankment for protection. Nine members of this group were from Lt Driskell's 1st Platoon; the other eight were with Sgt Williams from the Weapons Platoon. A few of Lt Driskell's men had already left but about 20, afraid to move across the flat paddies, had stayed behind. At the time, however, Driskell did not know what had happened to the rest of his platoon, so, after he had walked back to the vicinity of the group of houses behind the hill, he stopped at one of the rice-paddy trails to decide which way to go to locate his missing men. Just then someone walked past and told him that some of his men, including several who were wounded, were near the base of the hill. With one other man, Driskell went off to look for them.

33

'By the time the panicked riflemen of Company A had run the mile or two back to Pyongtaek they had overcome much of their initial fear. They gathered along the muddy main street of the village and stood there in the rain, waiting. When Capt Osburn arrived he immediately began assembling and reorganising his company for the march south. Meanwhile, men of Company C were waiting to dynamite the bridge at the north edge of the village. One of the officers found a jeep and trailer that had been abandoned on a side street. He and several of his men succeeded in starting it and, although it did not run well and had apparently been abandoned for that reason, they decided it would do for hauling the company's heavy equipment that was left. By 0930 they piled all extra equipment, plus the machine guns, mortars, bazookas, BARs and extra ammunition in the trailer. About the same time, several men noticed what appeared to be two wounded men trying to make their way along the road to Pyongtaek. It was still raining so hard that it was difficult to distinguish details. Pvt Thomas A. Cammarano and another man volunteered to take the jeep and go after them. They pulled a BAR from the weapons in the trailer, inserted a magazine of ammunition, and drove the jeep north across the bridge, not realising that the road was so narrow it would have been difficult to turn the vehicle around even if the trailer had not been attached.

'During the period when the company was assembling and waiting in Pyongtaek, Sgt Collins, the platoon sergeant who had joined the company the day before, decided to try to find out why his platoon had failed to fire effectively against the enemy. Of 31 members of his platoon, 12 complained that their rifles would not fire. Collins checked them and found that the rifles were either broken, dirty or had been assembled incorrectly. He sorted out the defective weapons and dropped them in a nearby well. Two other incidents now occurred that had an unfavourable effect on morale. The second shell fired by the North Koreans that morning had landed near Capt Osburn's CP where the observer for his 4.2in mortars was standing. The observer reached Pyongtaek while the men were waiting for Cammarano and his companion to return with the jeep. Suffering severely from shock, the mortar observer could not talk coherently and walked as if he were drunk. His eyes showed white, and he stared wildly, moaning, ''Rain, rain, rain,'' over and over again. About the same time, a member of the 1st Platoon joined the group and claimed that he had been with Lt Driskell after he had walked toward the cluster of houses searching for wounded men of his platoon. Lt Driskell with four men had been suddenly surrounded by a group of North Korean soldiers. They tried to surrender, according to his man, but one of the North Korean soldiers walked up to the lieutenant, shot him, and then killed the other three men. The narrator had escaped.

'Of the approximately 140 men who had been in position at daybreak that morning, only a few more than 100 were now assembled at Pyongtaek. In addition to the four men just reported killed, there were about 30 others who were missing. The first sergeant with eight men had followed a separate route after leaving the hill that morning and did not rejoin the company until several days later. One man failed to return after having walked down to a stream just after daylight to refill several canteens. There were also others who had been either afraid or unable to leave their foxholes to move back with the rest of the company. This group included the man from the listening post and about 20 members of 1st Platoon who had stayed in their holes in the rice paddies. Ten or fifteen minutes went by after Cammarano and his companion drove off in the jeep. Through the heavy rain and fog neither the jeep nor the wounded men were visible now. Suddenly there was the sound of rifle fire in the village and Capt Osburn, assuming that the two men (together with the vehicle and all the company crew-served weapons) were also lost, gave the word to move out. Forming the remainder of his company into two single-file columns, one on either side of the street, he started south. The men had scarcely reached the south edge of the village when they heard the explosion as the Company C men destroyed the bridge. One fourth of the company and most of its equipment and supplies were missing as the men set off on their forced march.'

The 24th Infantry Division had had a harsh initiation to warfare and they had seen only the beginning of fighting on the Korean peninsula. But when they again came to a halt beyond the Naktong River and turned to make another defensive stand against the North Koreans, they had ended the first phase of the Korean conflict. Other UN troops had arrived in Korea. The period of withdrawal was over. Members of Company A and the rest of the 34th Infantry had lost their overconfidence and gained battle experience. They soon settled down to a grim defence on the Pusan perimeter.

Defence of the Pusan perimeter

Under continual pressure the outnumbered and badly shaken US and ROK troops found themselves having to give up more and more ground as they were pushed further and further southwards. By the end of August the North Koreans appeared to be very near to complete victory. The UN forces had been squeezed into a small perimeter around the all-important port and supply base of Pusan (see map 3). Fortunately things were not quite as black as they appeared for the embattled defenders, thanks to the steady build-up of UN troops. The 25th Infantry and 1st Cavalry Divisions had arrived in the latter half of July to assist the 24th Infantry, and in August they were reinforced by the 2nd Infantry Division and US 1st Marine Brigade. All these formations were of course from the United States. In late August too the very first non-American troops arrived to swell the UN ranks, in the shape of the advance parties of the 27th British Infantry Brigade from Hong Kong. However, it was a desperate time for the UN command as they fought to retain a toe-hold on the peninsula. The US Eighth Army, as the UN forces were now called, were fortunate in having as their commander a tough, pugnacious Texan, Lt-Gen Walton H. Walker — nicknamed 'Johnny' after a famous brand of Scotch Whisky. Having served as one of Gen George S. Patton's corps commanders in his legendary US Third Army, Gen Walker was very much in the same mould as Patton. He believed in letting his soldiers see who was commanding them and left the day to day administration of his headquarters to his staff. Above all he was a fighter, and he let his men know that as far as he was concerned there would be no more 'bugging-out', no 'Dunkirk-type' rescue, and no surrender. They would hold the Pusan perimeter or die in the attempt.

To illustrate this perilous phase of the war I have chosen some extracts culled from the battle history of the US 25th Infantry Division entitled *Battleground Korea*.

The line holds

The 25th Division's new defences around Pusan had not been long completed when the North Koreans tested their strength. It was the 1st Battalion, 35th Regimental Combat Team that held the key to the vital Chungam-ni-Masan approach route. The enemy hit this unit first with an early morning barrage on 17 August, followed shortly afterwards by a savage attack on the forward positions. The leading platoons were forced to give ground, but then under covering fire from some well placed machine guns, a rifle company counterattacked and restored the lost positions to the Americans. The enemy, who had confidently moved up a large quantity of

Below: The Pusan perimeter.

Above: A US Army machine gun emplacement on the Pusan perimeter, September 1950. *UN (from US Army)*

heavy weapons and ammunition, was forced to abandon them and to flee, leaving many casualties. Next day they tried again, this time with a two-pronged assault on the 24th RCT as well as on the 35th. Some positions were taken, irrespective of casualties. One captured North Korean said that he was one of 2,000 civilians, who had been forced to march with the soldiers from the Seoul area in 10 long night marches. Each group of 10 civilians had a guard of two armed soldiers. He said that he had been pressed into service in a North Korean town and told that he was going to 'work in a factory' in some unknown destination in the south. Instead he and the others had been used to transport hand grenades from a supply dump in Seoul.

Typical of the bravery of the stubborn defenders is this extract from the citation of the posthumous award of the Congressional Medal of Honor, to Master Sergeant Melvin O. Handrich, a member of C Company, 5th Infantry Regiment who:
'Distinguished himself by conspicuous gallantry and intrepidity above and beyond the call of duty on 25 and 26 August 1950, near Sobuk-san Mountain, Korea. His company was engaged in repulsing an estimated 150 enemy who were threaten-

ing to overrun its position. Near midnight on 25 August, a hostile group of over 100 strong attempted to infiltrate the company perimeter. Sgt Handrich, despite heavy enemy fire, voluntarily left the comparative safety of the defensive area and moved to a forward position where he could direct mortar and artillery fire on to the advancing enemy. He remained at this post for eight hours, directing fire against the enemy who often approached within 50 feet of his position. With complete disregard for his safety, Sgt Handrich rose to his feet and from his exposed position fired his rifle and directed mortar and artillery fire on the attackers. At the peak of the action, he observed elements of his company preparing to withdraw. He perilously made his way across the fire-swept terrain to the defence area, where, by example and forceful leadership, he reorganised the men to continue to fight. During the action Sgt Handrich was severely wounded. Refusing to take cover or be evacuated, he returned to his forward position and continued to direct the company's fire. Later a determined attack by the enemy overran Sgt Handrich's position and he was mortally wounded. When the position was retaken, more than 70 enemy dead were counted in

Left: Men of US 9th Infantry Regiment aid a wounded soldier while under North Korean fire, September 1950. *UN (from US Army)*

the area he had so intrepidly defended. Sgt Handrich's sustained personal bravery, consummate courage, and gallant self-sacrifice reflect untold glory on himself and the heroic traditions of the military service.'

All three armed services played their part in the successful defence of the Masan-Pusan perimeter in those desperate days of August 1950. The US destroyers *Wiltsie* and *Endicott* effectively assisted the ground forces by denying the enemy large areas of the coast on the left front of the 25th Infantry Division. The enemy had built up a sizeable concentration of troops there, which the destroyers dispersed with their guns. The position had been described as a 'dagger' pointed at the Division's left flank, until this action by the US Navy dealt with it. The US Fifth Air Force also played its part in the coordinated fire control plan with the efficient use of fighters and bombers. They were directed by tactical air control parties at each regimental headquarters.

At this stage of the conflict personnel and supply problems were enormous — for example, four of the front line rifle companies of 25 Division had but one officer each. A few replacements were received

and some wounded were returned after a short period in hospital, nevertheless the combat effectiveness of the division was steadily reduced by the heavy attrition rate. As the history of the division put it: 'It was the old story — no matter how victorious US forces were, or how numerous the enemy slain — each victory cost the Americans casualties they could ill-afford. On the other hand, the enemy seemed to have an inexhaustible supply of manpower. To the Reds, the number of their casualties seemed to make no difference in the forces they were able to throw into battle. During the month, shortages of material resulting from combat losses began to rise to alarming totals. These shortages were particularly critical in ammunition, vehicles and signal equipment. The unsung heroes of the campaign were the men from the service elements and the various headquarters, who slaved long and weary hours to get supplies to the fighting men; administer to their wounds; and keep the records straight to ensure the support troops must have in order to function. Every American unit did its part to fit into the pattern.'

On 1 September, the North Korean Army made its most determined effort of the war, to break the Pusan perimeter and

Left: US Marines move past knocked out T-34/85 tanks, while South Korean civilians remove Marine dead, 18 August 1950. Note Bazooka teams carrying rockets and two-piece launchers.
US Marine Corps

Right and below: 105mm howitzers in action. Backbone of the American field artillery, was the M2A1, which had a maximum range of 12,500 yards and a shell weight of 33lb.
Royal Netherlands Embassy, London

occupy the coveted port. Their schedule called for its capture during the first six days of September and they launched a general offensive all around the Eighth Army defensive arc, with heavy attacks in all areas. On the 25 Division front in the first hour of the new month, the enemy struck with four regiments at once, at many places along the divisional front. Supported by artillery and tanks, hordes of Red troops hurled themselves at the Americans in wave after wave. But the division stuck to its positions, pouring devastating fire on to the attackers, until heaps of enemy dead lay in front of every position. The line bent, wavered at times, but held. On several occasions, companies were completely encircled by the enemy and cut off, but held their ground:

'In one case, a corporal assumed command of the remnants of his company after all its officers had become casualties. Later the young NCO told a story seldom matched — of his men hurling back Red grenades as fast as they came in — of grievously wounded comrades who suffered in silence so not to distract others from fighting off the attackers. One automatic rifleman, freshly arrived in Korea from his native Pennsylvania, worked his weapon coolly, refusing to stir from his position despite terrific enemy pressure. Afterwards, the bodies of 48 enemy were found in front of his post. He told newspaper men that he had learned to shoot as a child on his "daddy's farm", where as a boy he used to hunt squirrels. "Ammunition was pretty scarce in those days too", he reminisced. "We had to make every shot count".'

One amazing character of this period was a man known affectionately as 'The One Man Airforce'. Maj Dean Hess was an instructor with the embryo South Korean Air Force. At the time he had six P-51 Mustang fighter planes at his disposal, which were located not far from the 25 Division area. Hess kept the aircraft flying all round the clock. On one occasion, for example, he spotted an American ground patrol pinned down by enemy machine gun fire. He promptly flew low in front of the patrol, strafing the North Koreans at each pass and thus allowing the patrol to move a little closer to their own lines, each time the Reds took cover in their foxholes to avoid his fire. For every attack Hess made, the patrol got a little nearer home. By the time he had covered them all the way back, he was out of ammunition. He radioed for help to the Fifth Air Force, asking them to come and destroy the sizeable enemy force he had pinned down in no man's land. Even though his guns were now empty, he kept on buzzing them threateningly, as though looking for new targets. Eventually, however, they caught on and started to move back to their own lines. The quick-witted Hess, determined to hold the enemy in their exposed position at all costs until other planes arrived, didn't give up. Instead he pulled off one of his boots and dropped it into the middle of the enemy. Thinking that he had dropped a delayed-action bomb they immediately dived for cover. The other planes arrived just as he was tossing out his remaining

boot and Hess was able to return to his base, bootless but triumphant!

Another outstanding feat of heroism on the battlefield which probably saved many lives is also recorded in the 25 Division history, thus:

'Corporal Ervin H. Edwardsen, a Milwaukee infantrymen, brought a laden ammunition truck through a hail of bullets to bring new hope to an encircled company. The unit, surrounded by constantly attacking Reds, found itself facing annihilation through lack of cartridges with which to defend against the constant enemy attacks. The company would be shortly doomed unless cartridges could be gotten to them at once. When word of the company's plight reached the Battalion command post, Edwardsen volunteered to drive a load through to them. Shortly after setting out, he ran into a multiple machine gun fusilade and was forced back. Finding no alternate route, the determined American turned his truck around and backed at full speed through the storm of bullets. The road was narrow and the $2\frac{1}{2}$ton truck could not be turned, so Edwardsen continued in reverse gear for three miles. He ran one last deadly gauntlet of small arms fire, still in reverse. Then passing through the American defence perimeter at last, he reached his goal. He had brought the desperately needed ammunition through. Though unwounded himself, Edwardsen's truck was almost unsalvageable. It was riddled with bullet holes. Three tyres were shot away. The windscreen was shattered, and the truck was so badly riddled there was no repairing it. The ammunition boxes it carried had been penetrated many times by enemy slugs, but luckily none had exploded the ammunition. The Milwaukeean's act of daring brought the ammunition which enabled the company to fight its way out of the trap.'

Below: Infantrymen of 2 RAR, undergoing training at Puckapunyal, Victoria, October 1950. The tank is an M24 Chaffee. *Soldier*

To the Yalu!

Inchon

Since early August, Gen Douglas MacArthur had been planning the masterstroke that would break the deadlock around the Pusan perimeter and get the Eighth Army moving forward. The daring, imaginative plan which he subsequently evolved was typical 'MacArthur Magic' and very similar to those operations for which he had become justly famous in World War 2, namely an amphibious assault, deep in the enemy's rear. With complete superiority at sea and in the air, such a hazardous operation had a good chance of success. A completely new formation was set up in Japan for the landing — the US X Corps, which comprised two reinforced divisions, the US 7th Infantry and the US 1st Marine. The corps commander was Maj-Gen Edward M. Arnold and the complete operation would be under the control of Vice-Admiral Arthur R. Struble, commander of the US Seventh Fleet. Target for the operation was Inchon, on the west coast of Korea, in easy striking distance of the South Korean capital of Seoul. It was a bold plan, which was to prove stunningly successful. The landing was effected on 15 September and the port of Inchon captured the same day. From Inchon, Gen Arnold's troops drove east and south to block the approaches to Seoul which was garrisoned by a North Korean

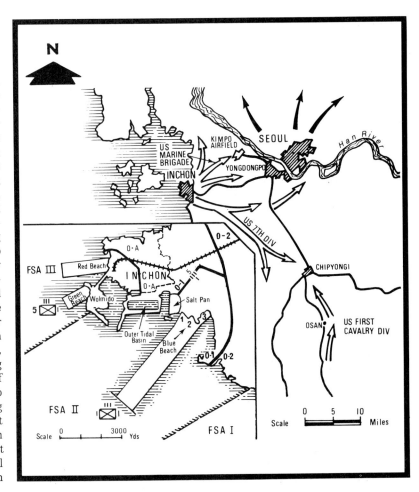

Above: The Inchon landings, 15 September 1950.

Left: Leathernecks use scaling ladders to storm ashore at Inchon, 15 September 1950.
US Marine Corps

division. One Marine column captured Yongdungpo, an industrial suburb south of the Han River, while another seized Kimpo airfield. Just two days later the airfield was in operation again, handling vital cargoes flown in from Japan. The men of the US 7th 'Bayonet' Division which had landed behind the Marines, drove south to Suwon, taking the town and its airfield on 22 September. On the same day, the US 1st Cavalry Division burst out of the Pusan perimeter and started north, linking up with the advancing 7th Division infantrymen on 26 September at Osan. Seoul fell the same day, after some very bitter hand to hand fighting, with the Marines having to winkle out the stubborn defenders block by block. The end of the war must have looked very close to the men of the victorious United Nations forces, as they got ready to cross the 38th Parallel in pursuit of the shattered North Korean Army.

The Inchon landing provides a good opportunity to salute the bravery of that world famous fighting man, the United States Marine, although the USMC had of course been in action much earlier, as the US 1st Provisional Marine Brigade was ordered to Korea in early July and the first Marines actually landed at Pusan on 2 August. For this short tribute I have chosen accounts of part of the initial assault landing at Inchon, which are contained in the official history, the *US Marine Operations in Korea 1950-53* and are published here with kind permission of the Headquarters US Marine Corps. As the map shows, there were to be landings on three beaches: *Red Beach* — 5th Marine Regiment (less one battalion) would land at Red Beach and plunge into the dense waterfront area of the sprawling seaport, their mission being to seize the line O-A, a 3,000-yard arc from Cemetery Hill in the north, to Observatory Hill in the centre and thence extending for the last 1,000 yards through a maze of buildings and streets to end at the inner tidal basin. *Green Beach* — Prior to the main assault, 3/5 Battalion would land at Green Beach on Wolmi-do. *Blue Beach* — Finally, some three miles to the south-east, 1st Marines would seize Blue Beach, a north-south strip fronting a suburban industrial area. Let us first look at the initial landings on Wolmi-do by the 3/5 Battalion:

'The pre-dawn stillness of the Yellow Sea was shattered as the Corsairs of Marine Fighter Squadrons VMF-214 and VMF-323 flashed up from the decks of the *Sicily* and *Badeong Strait*. To the west the planes of Task Force 77 were assembling in attack formation above the *Valley Forge*,

Above: Enemy bunkers are demolished by grenades and planted charges.
UN (from Department of Defense)

Philippine Sea and *Boxer*. Squadron after squadron droned eastwards through the blackness and the first aircraft began orbiting over the objective area at 0454. Two hours earlier, Advance Attack Group 90.1, under Capt Norman W. Sears USN, had glided into the entrance of Flying Fish Channel. Led by the *Mansfield* the column of 19 ships snaked through the treacherous passage while captains and navigators sweated over radar scopes. Lt Clark's handiwork* provided a welcome relief midway along the route, where the glimmering beacon on Palmi-do guided vessels past one of the more dangerous. points in the channel. Minutes after air cover began to form over Inchon, the ships eased into the narrows west of Wolmi-do and sought assigned battle stations. Training their big guns on the port city were the cruisers *Toledo*, *Rochester*, *Kenya* and *Jamaica*, comprising one of the three fire support units under Adm Higgins. Other support vessels scattered throughout the waters were the destroyers *Collet*, *Gurke*, *Henderson*, *Mansfield*, *De Haven*, *Swenson* and *Southerland*; and this array of firepower was further supplemented by three bristling rocket ships. The control ship, *Mount McKinley* its flag bridge crowded with star studded commanders,

* Lt Eugene F. Clark, a naval officer on MacArthur's staff had gone ashore on Yonghungho island about 15 miles SW of Inchon some days before the assault. He had recruited a 'private army' to help him report on enemy movements and, on 14 September, had managed to light the lighthouse on Palmi island which had been put out of action by the enemy. It was the former entrance beacon for Inchon via Flying Fish Channel. He received a Silver Star for his daring exploits.

Left: US Marines launch a
4.5in rocket barrage.
US Marine Corps

Below: Marine riflemen stand
by as their 3.5in bazooka man
puts a round into a Communist
position. *US Marine Corps*

steamed into the narrows just before dawn. No sooner had the grey shoreline become outlined in the morning haze than the 6 and 8-inch guns of the cruisers belched sheets of orange flame in the direction of Inchon and at 0545, the initial explosions rocked the city and reverberated throughout the channel. There was a deafening crescendo as the destroyers hammered Wolmi-do with their 5-inch guns. Radio Hill, its seaward side already burnt and blackened from previous bombardments was almost hidden by smoke when Marine planes streaked down at 0600 to smother the island with tons of rockets and bombs. Capt Sears, reporting to the *Mount McKinley*, confirmed L-hour at 0630. To this end Lt-Col Robert D. Taplett's landing force was boated by 0600, and the LCVPs (Landing Craft Vehicle and Personnel) and LSUs (Landing Ship Utility) rendezvoused while the Marine air arm continued to soften up the target.

'Air attacks ceased at 0615, but Wolmi-do enjoyed only a momentary respite before the most unnerving blow of all. In strange contrast to the sleek man-o'-war and nimble aircraft, three squat LSMRs (Landing Ship, Medium Rocket) closed in on the island from the north a few hundred yards offshore. Phalanxes of rockets arose from the decks of the clumsy ships, arched steeply and crashed down. One of the rocket ships, taking a southerly course, passed Green Beach and dumped salvo after salvo along the slopes and crest of Radio Hill. When the LSMR cleared North Point of Wolmi-do, seven LCVPs darted across the line of departure and sped shoreward with 3rd Battalion, 5th Marines first wave. Rockets and 40mm shells were still ripping the southern half of the island when one platoon of Company G and three platoons of Company H stormed Green Beach at 0633. Two minutes later, the second wave of landing craft ground to a halt on the sand, bringing the remainder of both assault companies. The Marines were confronted by a scene of devastation almost devoid of enemy resistance. Only a few scattered shots greeted the assault force as it punched inland. The failure of the Underwater Demolitions Team (UDT) men to clear away all the wrecked craft cluttering the beach had left 3/5 a landing strip less than 50 yards wide. Consequently, each wave had to contract like an accordion, and there was considerable crowding during the first crucial minutes of the landing. But even at this stage, the potent Marine air arm offered a final measure of protection to the infantrymen splashing ashore. Pilots swung their F4Us 50 yards ahead of the assault troops and

44

Right: Seizure of Wolmi-do by 3/5 Marines, 15 September 1950.

Left: Leathernecks with M26 tank support were involved in bitter street fighting in Seoul. *Patton Museum*

Below left: British Royal Marine commandos worked closely with the USMC. Here they are carrying out a daring raid near Songjin in North Korea to destroy enemy supply lines. The amtracks are operated by US Marines. *UN (from US Navy)*

Below: Commandos of 41st Commando inspect damage done to a stretch of railway track, eight miles south of Songjin, North Korea, April 1951. *UN (from US Navy)*

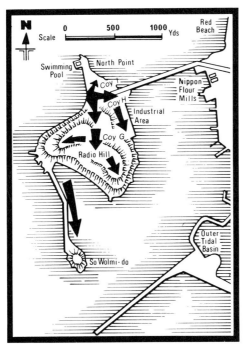

hosed the routes of advance with machine gun bullets. After a brief pause for reorganisation at the beach, 1-Lt Robert D. Bohn's Company G wheeled to the right and drove up the northern slopes of Radio Hill, Objective 1-A. Only half-hearted resistance was met along the way, most of the scattered and numb North Koreans preferring to surrender rather than face the inevitable. At 0655, Sgt Alvin E. Smith, guide of the 3rd Platoon, secured the American flag to a shell-torn tree on the crest. At this point Gen MacArthur rose from the swivel chair in which he had been viewing the operation on the flag bridge of the *Mount McKinley*. ''That's it'', he said, ''Let's get a cup of coffee.''

'Meanwhile, the Wolmi-do assault continued as Capt Patrick E. Wildman, after detaching a small force from Company H to clear the rubble-strewn North Point, attacked across Wolmi-do toward the Inchon causeway with the rest of his unit. H Company's mission was to seize Objec-

45

tive 2-B, which included the eastern nose of Radio Hill and the shore-line industrial area facing Inchon. At 0646, the three LSUs comprising the third wave, squeezed into the narrow beach and disgorged the armoured detachment of Company A, 1st Tank Battalion, under 2-Lt Granville G. Sweet. Ten tanks were landed in all — six M26s, one flamethrower, two dozers and one retriever. The big vehicles crunched inland a short distance to await calls from the infantry. Lt-Col Taplett ordered his free boat to beach at 0650. Fifteen minutes later he radioed the *Mount McKinley* and *Fort Marion* that his assault companies were advancing on schedule. It was ironic that 3/5s reserve company should encounter the angriest hornet's nest of Wolmi-do. Landing in the fourth wave at 0659, Capt Robert A. McMullen's Company I moved through North Point in trace of the H Company detachment which supposedly had cleared the area. Suddenly a flurry of hand grenades clattered on the rubble, and the surprised Marines scattered for cover. Regaining their composure after the explosions, the infantrymen determined the source of trouble to be a bypassed string of enemy emplacements dug into a low cliff at the shoreline, facing Inchon. There appeared to be a platoon of North Koreans, who would rise from their holes inter-

mittently, fling grenades inland, then disappear from sight. I Company's interpreter crawled toward the cliff during a lull, bellowing to the Reds that their predicament was hopeless and exhorting them to surrender. When the Communists responded to this advice by throwing more grenades, McMullen signalled Sweet's tanks into action. The M26s and Marine riflemen took covering positions, while the dozer tank, directed by McMullen himself, rumbled into the troublesome pocket and systematically sealed the die-hard Reds into their holes. Another bit of drama unfolded before the reserve troops when they closed on the causeway terminus in the wake of H Company's advance. From one of the caves drifted noises indicating the presence of several occupants, hitherto unnoticed. While riflemen covered the entrance, a Marine tank drove forward and fired two rounds into the interior. Muffled explosions shook the area, and billows of black smoke streaked with flame, rolled out of the cave. Wide-eyed, as though watching ghosts emerge, the Marines of Company I saw 30 enemy soldiers stagger out of the blazing recess and throw up their hands.

'Less than an hour after landing 3/5 controlled half of Wolmi-do. Company H, having cleared the causeway terminus, was

Below: Men and equipment of the 2nd Infantry Division wait to cross the Hwang-gang River, during the UN offensive, 25 September 1950. Note the Russian-made SU-76 self propelled anti-tank gun on right of picture. *US Army*

pivoting southward to clean out the ruins of the industrial area. Engineers, close on the heels of the infantry, advanced 25 yards out on the pavement leading to Inchon and laid an anti-tank minefield. Company G had advanced about 400 yards and was clearing the northern crest of Radio Hill. Action up to this point is best summed up in Taplett's message to the *Mount McKinley* at 0745: "Captured 45 prisoners. Meeting light resistance." Nor did the situation change as Company G occupied the dominating peak of Radio Hill, some 105 metres high. The enemy lacked the will to fight, despite the fact that he had sufficient weapons and a formidable defensive complex from which to fire them. Frightened, dejected Red soldiers continued to surrender singly or in small groups, and Taplett exulted over the amazingly light casualties sustained by his battalion. Since Company H found the going slow in the shambles of the industrial area, the battalion commander ordered Lt Bohn to seize the whole of Radio Hill. Accordingly, G Company troops rushed across the ridgeline to the eastern spur. This done, Bohn despatched a force to clear the western reaches of the high ground. By 0800, Radio Hill became the property of the 1st Marine Division, and with the prize went control of the island and Inchon Harbour. When the news of 3/5's success blared from the loudspeaker on the flag bridge of the *Mount McKinley* the commander in chief, wearing his famous leather jacket and braided campaign cap, withdrew to his cabin and penned a spirited message to Vice-Admiral Struble aboard the *Rochester*: "The Navy and Marines have never shone more brightly than this morning. MACARTHUR."

'Consolidation of Wolmi-do required the reduction of an enemy outpost on Sowolmi-do, the small lighthouse station connected to the southwestern tip of the island by a causeway 750 yards long and 12 yards wide. An islet of about 500 yards square, Sowolmi-do was topped by a low hill with the navigational beacon on the summit. Before bothering with this tiny, isolated target, Taplett put his larger house in order. By previous plan, the three rifle companies of 3/5 took up defensive positions facing Inchon. I Company occupied North Point, Wildman's unit the slopes above the industrial area, and Company G the crest of Radio Hill. While the battalion dug in, mopping-up operations throughout the island continued to net more prisoners and reveal the extent of North Korean fortifications. Radio Hill was ringed by mutually supporting trenches and emplacements, all of which had brought

only negligible return to the Reds' investment in time and labour. Parked on the western nose of the ridge were two intact 76mm anti-tank guns that could have wrought havoc on landing waves approaching Green Beach. Fortunately, these weapons had been exposed to the 40mm rocket fire of the LSMR covering the beach assault, and their crews lacked the stomach to man them. More anti-tank guns were scattered around the terminus of the causeway leading to Inchon, leaving some questions as to whether they had been rushed to the defence of the island or were marked for displacement to the city. North Point, once a luxurious resort, was honeycombed with caves used both for storage and for bomb shelters. The swimming pool, one of the few structures still recognisable after the bombardment, was converted by the Marines into a POW stockade. More than 300 cast-iron anti-personnel mines were found attached to the barbed wire entanglement stretched along the west coast at the base of Radio Hill. The explosives were removed and disarmed by T/Sgt Edwin L. Knox and his detachment from Company A, 1st Engineer Battalion. Though the North Koreans had been helpful in placing these mines in so obvious a location, they had, oddly enough, failed to employ similar obstacles on the

Below: No caption needed!
UN

Far left: Men of the 1st Battalion, The Middlesex Regiment, which landed in Korea in August 1950 as part of 27th Brigade, move up to the front as the UN troops advance from the Pusan perimeter. *IWM*

Left: Men of the Middlesex Regiment pass three US M4A3s engaging the enemy. *UN (from US Army)*

beaches, roads, and paths around the island.

'Prior to the midmorning advance on Sowolmi-do, total casualties from the 3rd Battalion were 14 wounded — an incredibly small price to pay for a critical terrain feature commanding the approaches to Korea's major west coast port. Evacuation plans so carefully laid out by the 1st Medical Battalion worked smoothly. In the early phases of the operation, LCVPs returning from Green Beach delivered Marine casualties to the *Fort Marion*, whose normal medical complement had been augmented by a special surgical team. Men with particularly bad wounds were transferred to the *Mount McKinley* after being administered first aid. As the battle developed, navy corpsmen of 3/5 established a collecting point on a small pier which could be reached by ambulance boats even during low water. Shortly before 1000, Taplett ordered Company G to seize Sowolmi-do. Both in turn assigned the mission to one infantry squad reinforced with machine guns and a section of tanks, all under the control of 2-Lt John D. Counselman, leader of G Company's 3rd Platoon. Although the islet was by no means an objective of formidable proportions, the attackers eyed their route of approach over the long strip with misgivings. Their scepticism was not unfounded, for they neared the entrance to the causeway only to be stopped cold by heavy rifle and machine gun fire from the other end. A platoon of North Koreans, almost literally at the end of their rope, preferred to fight it out. Taplett ordered the tank-infantry team to hold up while he radioed a mission to Marine air. A few minutes later, Corsairs of VMF-214 nosed down and scorched the objective with napalm. Sweet's tanks, preceded by an engineer mine-clearance team and followed by the column of infantrymen, rumbled on to the rock bed tracing the seaward edge of the causeway. As the task force filed across the exposed route, 81mm mortar shells from 3/5s mortar platoon rattled overhead and tore into the Communist emplacements. Enemy fire was reduced to a light patter, and the observers on Radio Hill breathed a sigh of relief when the attackers gained the far end of the causeway at 1048. Covered by tank fire, the Marine infantry quickly fanned out and closed with the defenders. There was a sharp outburst of small-arms racket, interspersed with the clatter of machine guns: then a few scattered volleys and the main fight was over at 1115. Mopping up with grenades and a flamethrower continued for almost another hour, owing to the number of caves and the determination of a few Red soldiers. Nine North Korean soldiers surrendered and 17 were killed, including some hapless warriors who tried to swim to the mainland. Despite the size of the islet, eight Reds succeeded in hiding out from the attackers; and Gen Craig, after landing on Wolmi-do with the Advanced Divisional Command Group in the evening, observed the fugitives escape to the mainland.'

The afternoon of 15 September wore on, while the mainland remained fairly quiet. Then, following another massive air and sea bombardment, the main assault on to Red and Blue Beaches began — H-hour was 1730. The Marine history explains:
'The critical moment of every amphibious assault was now at hand — the moment when intelligence and planning would be put to the test of actuality. On the bridge of the *Mount McKinley* high-ranking Army, Navy and Marine Corps officers gathered again about Gen MacArthur, seated in a swivel chair. They listened for the second time that day as the loudspeaker gave a blow-by-blow account of the developments

reported by aerial observers. Everything
that air attacks and naval gunfire could do
to soften up the target had been done, yet
no one could be sure just what sort of
opposition the troops would encounter in
Red and Blue Beaches. It might be
fainthearted as that brushed aside by the
3/5 on Wolmi-do; or it might be that
another Tarawa awaited on those cramped
strips of urban waterfront lying between
the mudflats of the harbour and the dark
crooked streets of the Asiatic town and
environs. The enemy had been given ample
time in which to prepare for a defence of
the mainland. . . With H-hour only minutes
away, the sky above the objective was
murky and the wind whipped rain as well
as stinging spray into the faces of the
Marines in the assault waves. Only the
Marine and Navy fliers upstairs could see
the panorama of the waterborne attack —
the cruisers and destroyers standing silent
in the background, LSMR rocket flashes
stabbing the false twilight ashore, the
landing craft trailing pale wakes behind
them like the trails of comets. The pilots
observed the LCVPs to the left of Wolmi-do
fan out at the line of departure and touch
the sea wall of Red Beach minutes later. To
the right of the little island, however, they
saw the leading waves of the 1st Marines
disappear into a blanket of gloom.

'For a while the smoke and moisture
laden air had obscured parts of the 5th
Marines zone of action ashore, it had also
completely blotted out Blue Beach and half
the length of the 1st Regiment's boat
lanes. . . On the north of Red Beach, three
of the four LCVPs with the leading elements of Company A bumped the sea wall
at 1733. Boat number one, carrying T/Sgt

Orval F. McMullen and half of his 1st
Platoon, was delayed off-shore by an
engine failure. The remainder of the 1st,
under the platoon guide, Sgt Charles D.
Allen, scaled the wall from boat number
two in the face of heavy fire from the north
flank and from sub-machine guns in a
bunker directly ahead. Several Marines
were cut down immediately, the others
being unable to advance more than a few
yards inland. Boat number three, with 2-Lt
Francis W. Muetzel and a squad of his 2nd
Platoon, touched a breach in the sea wall
under the muzzle of an enemy machine gun
protruding from a pillbox. The weapon did
not fire as the Marines scrambled through
the gap and on to the beach. A second
squad and a 3.5in rocket section joined
from boat number four. Gunfire crackled
far off on the left, barely audible amid the
roar of fighter planes strafing 50 yards
ahead. Muetzel and his men jumped into a
long trench which paralleled the sea wall a
few feet away. It was empty. Two Marines
threw grenades into the silent pillbox, and
the six bloody North Koreans who emerged
in the wake of the hollow explosions were
left under guard of a Marine rifleman.

'Just beyond the beach loomed
Cemetery Hill, its seaward side an almost
vertical bluff. To avoid getting trapped if
the enemy opened up from the high
ground, Muetzel attacked towards his
objective, the Asahi Brewery, without
waiting for the remainder of his men in the
tardy second wave. The skirmish line
raced across the narrow beach, ignoring
padlocked buildings and flaming
wreckage. Passing to the south of
Cemetery Hill, the 2nd Platoon entered the
built-up area of the city and marched up a

street to the brewery. On the left of Company A's zone, the beached half of the 1st Platoon made no progress against the flankings fire and the Communist bunker to the front. The 3rd Platoon under 1-Lt Baldemero Lopez, landed in the second wave, and McMullen finally got ashore with the other half of the 1st. Both units crowded into the restricted foothold and casualties mounted rapidly. Enemy guns felled Lopez as he climbed ashore and moved against the bunker with a grenade. Unable to throw the armed missile because of his wound, the young officer was killed as he smothered the explosion with his body to protect his men. Two marines attacked the emplacement with flamethrowers. They were shot down and their valuable assault weapons put out of action. The situation on the left was at its worst when Capt Stevens landed in Muetzel's zone at H plus 5. Learning of Lopez's death and unable to contact McMullen, he ordered his executive officer, 1-Lt Fred F. Eubanks, Jr, to "Take over on the left and get them organised and moving." Time was of the essence, since Cemetery Hill, objective of the 1st Platoon, still remained in enemy hands. Succeeding waves would be landing hundreds of Marines in the shadow of the cliff within the next half hour. Stevens also radioed Muetzel, whose small force had reached the brewery without suffering a casualty, and ordered the 2nd Platoon back to the beach to help out.

'Muetzel immediately formed up his unit in column and struck out on the return trip to the waterfront. Nearing Cemetery Hill again, he noted that the southern slope of the vital objective was an excellent route to the top. In planning Company A's part of the operation, Stevens had once told him that the 2nd Platoon could expect to help seize the high ground if the job proved too rough for the 1st alone. With a creditable display of judgement and initiative, Muetzel launched an assault on the key to Red Beach. The Marines moved rapidly up the incline, flushing out about a dozen Red soldiers who surrendered meekly. Gaining the summit, they drove forward and saw the entire crest come alive with infantry-crewmen of the 226th NKPA Regiment's mortar company. Spiritless and dazed from the pounding by air and naval gunfire, the North Koreans to a man threw down their weapons, filed quietly from trenches and bunkers, and marched to the base of the hill where a small detachment kept them under guard. Hardly a shot had been fired by the 2nd Platoon, still without a single casualty, and the capture of Cemetery Hill had required about 10 minutes. During the

attack on the high ground, Eubanks had taken the situation in hand on the left of the beach. He first bested the bunker's occupants in a grenade duel, then ordered the emplacement fired by a flamethrower. Just as Muetzel prepared to despatch assistance from the top of Cemetery Hill, the 1st and 3rd Platoons broke out of the pocket, drove inland to the edge of the city, and made physical contact with the 2nd. At 1755, Stevens fired an amber cluster signifying that Cemetery Hill was secured for the 5th Marines. The half-hour fight in the north corner of Red Beach had cost Company A eight killed and 28 wounded.'

While the 5th Marines were battling to secure their objectives on Red Beach, 1st Marines were engaged in similar tasks on Blue Beach. Here is just a fragment of the narrative of their assault:

'The nine LVT(A)s comprising 3/1s first wave had closed on the sea wall of Blue Beach Two shortly after H-hour. Nosing their vehicles toward the drainage ditch on the left, drivers apparently eyed the muck and confirmation of the restricted passageway with some scepticism, for they backed off and exchanged fire with scattered enemy soldiers shooting from just beyond the waterfront. Wave number two passed through the Army tractors and bumped the sea wall ten minutes late with the leading Companies G and I, the former on the left. Since the landing echelons had intermingled in the cloudy boat lane, some LVTs of the third wave arrived with those of the second. This accounted for Lt Col Ridge's tractor reaching the beach one increment ahead of schedule. The battalion commander and his executive officer, Maj Reginald R. Myers, immediately swung their separate vehicles around the right flank, Ridge heading toward the ramp while the other officer continued around the corner in the direction of Blue Three. On the left of Blue Two, meanwhile, the amphibians carrying Capt George C. Westover's Company G formed a column and crawled into the drainage ditch. Troops of 1-Lt Joseph R. Fisher's I Company simultaneously scrambled up their aluminium ladders and deployed just beyond the sea wall in the face of moderate small arms fire. As had been anticipated, some of the metal scaling devices bent and buckled under the strain, delaying troop debarkation from the landing craft crowding the revetment. Assault elements of Capt Lester G. Harmon's Company C, 1st Engineer Bn, reached the beach and anchored cargo nets over the wall to speed up the landing. The lead tractor of G Company's column bellied down in the mud of

the drainage ditch, blocking five other LVTs behind. Westover ordered his troops to dismount and move forward along a road near the beach. After a brief period of reorganisation, Company G fanned out for the drive inland, its mission being to block a lowland corridor and secondary access road leading to Blue Beach out of the east... Despite the initial delays at the ditch and sea wall, Companies G and I cleared the beach rapidly. Of the few casualties taken in the first 30 minutes ashore, most were caused by an enemy machine gun in a tower about 500 yards inland. LVT fire silenced the weapon, and the Marine infantrymen plunged forward through a labyrinth of blazing buildings and smoke-filled streets... While the assault units fought inland, the gathering darkness created one more formidable handicap for the last wave serials leaving the line of departure far out in the channel... Since current and smoke fought relentlessly against tractors seaward of the line of departure, not all of the vehicles could find the control ship. If they did, it was next to impossible to come in close enough to get instructions shouted from the bridge. Thus many wave commanders, amtrac (amphibian tractor) officers and infantry leaders gave orders to head shoreward on their own initiative. They went in with waves and fragments of waves, displaying the kind of leadership that made the operation an overwhelming success in spite of the obstacles. This was the case with the three waves of 2/1 that failed to arrive at Blue One. They found their way ashore, some of the LVTs landing on Blue Two, others diverted to Blue Three; but the important thing was that they got there.'

Breakout from the Pusan Perimeter

As explained, in concert with the spectacular X Corps landings at Inchon, the Eighth Army launched an all out offensive to break free of the Pusan perimeter beginning on 16 September. Initially they met stiff resistance, but this did not last for long and once the advance really got under way, with IX US Corps leading, it pushed rapidly northwards. By the end of September UN forces had just about cleared all the remnants of the enemy out of South Korea. Having made the difficult decision to cross the 38th Parallel, the race for the Yalu began in earnest. British and Commonwealth troops were now taking part in the fighting, with the British Commonwealth 27 Infantry Brigade (comprising 1st Middlesex, 1st Argyll & Sutherland Highlanders and the 3rd Royal Australian Regiment), under command of first the 24th US Infantry Division up to Kallung and then of the US 1st Cavalry Division. As they lacked supporting arms and services, Brig Aubrey Coad, the brigade commander, had to scrounge from the Eighth Army, American artillery, engineers and part of the 89th Medium Tank Battalion. The combined force was under the operational control of the 1st Cavalry Division, but worked mainly as a separate task force, because of the nature of their tasks and the distances involved. These operations provide a good example of the excellent cooperation between the members of the United Nations Command.

I have chosen two short stories taken from accounts of 27 Brigade activities during the advance, the first being the very strange action fought by the Argylls at Sariwon. It was not their first battle in Korea, they had already taken part in fighting around the Pusan perimeter in early September, while their capture and subsequent action on Hill 282, had resulted in the posthumous award of the Victoria Cross to Maj Kenny Muir. It was on 15 October that they crossed the 38th Parallel and entered North Korea. The following day Brig Coad received orders that the brigade was to pass through the leading units of 1st Cavalry Division at dawn on the 17th and take over the lead on the main axis and most direct route to Pyongyang. 1st Argylls were to lead the brigade advance, their initial objective being the town of Sariwon, which was described as being the North Korean equivalent of Aldershot, about 30 miles ahead. A simultaneous advance on the town was to be made by the US 24th Infantry Division, in the form of a left hook, coming in on Sariwon from the west. It was soon apparent to the Argylls that what was happening here was actually a contest between the 1st Cavalry Division and the 24th Infantry Division, to see who could be first into the town. Maj (now Brig) David Wilson was commanding A Company of the Argylls who were the initial advanced guard. He writes:

'By the middle of October 1950, it was clear that North Korean resistance was becoming very disorganised and on the 16th 1 A&SH, reinforced by elements of the US 89th Tank Battalion, was ordered to drive north towards Pyongyang, via Sinmak and Sariwon. A Company was to be in the lead. The drive to Sinmak from Kaesong was uneventful, but at least it allowed us to have a day's practice with our tanks. One difficulty was that we had no wireless that could work on the tank net, but the problem was solved by putting on each platoon leader's tank an Argyll signaller with a WS88 on the company net, plus a pick-helve to hammer on the turret top to attract attention should the tank be closed down! Soon after first light on the 17th we started forward from Sohung, in what was a reasonable formation for an advanced guard — one platoon of tanks with infantry on board, Coy HQ, medium machine gun section, mortar section, artillery FOO (Forward Observation Officer) and the remainder of the company with another platoon of tanks. There was also a small recce detachment of US engineers.

'There was little or no resistance for the first 10 miles apart from a small hold-up in one village where Pte Kinne was killed by sniping (his brother Derek Kinne of the Royal Northumberland Fusiliers, was later to win the George Cross for valiant conduct as a POW), and by midafternoon we were approaching Sariwon. By then, however, the order of march had change a bit. Ahead and above the column was a light aeroplane in which was flying the 89th Tank Battalion commander, who was giving orders and encouragement to his leading platoon of tanks. Behind Coy HQ had infiltrated sundry vehicles, one containing a distinguished, but somewhat elderly US Army major-general, who was one of the President's personal liaison officers in Korea. Another jeep contained a colonel from 1 US Corps, whose role at that stage was not quite clear. Then followed the World Press — about six of them with cameras, ready to snap our every move. The first contretemps occurred when, during a halt to inspect a bridge that might have been mined, the General shot a Korean chicken with his pistol. The advanced guard, hearing the report thought there was a sniper about, debussed and was about to leap into action, when we realised what had happened. I would dearly loved to have told the general what to do with his pistol, but we did manage to impress on him to reserve the remainder of his ammunition for something more worthwhile than chickens. The advance continued, until about three miles south of Sariwon when we were shot at from a low ridge to the left of the road and some sort of light anti-tank shell hit the lead tank. Obviously the ridge had to be cleared and it was a simple matter to get the leading platoon, supported by tank, mortar and MMG fire, to attack it from the flank. Unfortunately, the somewhat odd composition of the advanced guard posed

certain hazards. The Tank Battalion CO, who thought he had better ideas from "on high", ordered his tanks to: "Barrel through", not realising that his lead tank couldn't move and was blocking the road. When he did realise it, he and his light aircraft landed on the road in front of Coy HQ and the MMGs, to add to the fun. The World Press, eager to get some good action pictures, clustered around the mortars, with shouts of: "Hold it!" just as a bomb was going down the barrel, the better to get a picture. Despite these "hazards", the attack which took the position from a flank, was completely successful, I think we only had three casualties, but counted some 40 enemy dead and captured eight LMGs. Had we arrived an hour or so later, it might have not been so easy. Leslie Neilson, my CO, very rightly realised that my company was now spread out all over the countryside, and told me to halt and consolidate, while the rest of 1 A&SH went through. At this moment the colonel from I Corps took a hand. It was essential, he said, that A Company should not waste time waiting for the others to pass through, but should press on boldly into Sariwon, so as to arrive before the 24th Division who were coming from the left. 1st Cavalry Division would then get a clear road ahead to

Below: 'Deuce and a half' trucks and jeeps, move out Leathernecks of the 1st Marine Division. *US Marine Corps*

Below: Leathernecks engaging the advancing Chinese onslaught in North Korea, the marines were eventually successfully withdrawn by sea. *US Marine Corps*

Right: A billow of smoke and flame rises as US Marine Corps fighters engage enemy positions with napalm. *US Army photo for UN*

Pyongyang, and be first there just as they had been first into Manila and Tokyo five years before. Fortunately, before there was time for a crisis of discipline and loyalty to develop, the remainder of the battalion and 3 RAR swept through, Sariwon was ours and so was the road to Pyongyang. Alas despite our efforts 1st Cavalry Division didn't win the race to Pyongyang. The 6th ROK Division, coming up on their right over the hills, just beat them to it!'

B Company (Maj Gordon-Ingram) now passed through A and were given the near (ie the southern) end of Sariwon as their objective by Col Leslie Neilson DSO, who now takes up the story:

'B Coy were to establish themselves firmly. Once this was done — against no opposition — C Coy (Maj Gillies) was ordered through to the north end of the town with a similar role, and Battalion HQ moved to the town centre pulling B Coy behind it. In the course of these moves, Brigade ordered the 3rd Royal Australian Regiment right through Sariwon, to take up a position astride the road to the north. All this was accomplished without difficulty or casualties. Sariwon itself was a complete ruin, as a result, no doubt of repeated bombing, and the ruins appeared to be full of disorganised North Korean soldiers. Firing was fairly heavy, but, quite remarkably, no one was getting hit. However, it did not seem to me that much could be achieved in the town overnight and, as it was secure, I contemplated suggesting to the Brigadier that a more restful night might be assured for those of us in the middle of the town if we withdrew to the outskirts until morning — evening was approaching by now — and then cleaned the place up properly in the daylight. The Brigadier, however, had other ideas.

'As I have already said, the 24th Infantry Division was due to enter Sariwon from the west, and he wished me to look at the road up which they would come to sweep into the net any North Koreans who might be withdrawing in front of them. Wishing to keep B Coy as a firm base, and with the Australians now in position to the north, I withdrew C Coy from the far edge of Sariwon. Their's was the blocking job and I assembled a reconnaissance party accordingly. For vehicles I took my landrover (it had been shipped specially from Hong Kong with the battalion Bren carrier). We moved off, but had hardly gone 30 or 40 yards in a northerly direction, before turning down the road towards the west, when a North Korean truck containing some 20 North Koreans swung in from that very road and, in error, turned towards my recce party and B Coy. They immediately realised that they were in trouble and the shooting started. My party was in worse difficulty, sandwiched between the two. We baled out very smartly and ran for cover, and never have my feet felt more leaden, the bullets kicking up the dust around my heels. It was like a bad dream. However, I reached a small wooden house and found myself there with one private soldier, one of my escort no doubt. And then again, as in a bad dream, I heard that North Korean truck coming slowly towards me, until it stopped right bang outside our window. My companion had a Sten gun, but this managed to jam most effectively and my skill was even less than his in dealing with it. Meanwhile our little wooden house was becoming somewhat porous from the shots B Coy directed at the truck, so there was nothing for it but an ignominious retreat by the back door and thence to battalion HQ as fast as I could make it. By the time I got there, however, the battle was over. Someone had thrown a grenade into the back of the truck and that was that — about 20 North Koreans dead and again no Argyll casualties. So we dusted ourselves down and set off again on that reconnaissance.

'Presently we reached the edge of the town which just petered out in a scatter of small houses and huts, the ground absolutely flat and offering no suitable position for my pupose. I was therefore about to turn round and settle for a second best, closer to Sariwon, when I became aware that we were no longer alone. Advancing towards us in single file on each side of the road were a large number of soldiers, stretching back along the road as far as I could see. They were clearly not Americans and there were no South Koreans within miles; they were in fact North Koreans, driven before the advancing 24th US Infantry. Small things stick in one's mind and I remember thinking how long their bayonets were; they had them stuck on their rifles for some reason. As soon as they saw us the first few files brought their rifles down and had a bang at us, but I had the presence of mind — or something — to shout to our chaps not to shoot. To try and bluff it out was the only way. This proved to be rather a puzzlement to the other side who, as it turned out — they were all put in the bag by the Australians — came to the conclusion that we were the forerunners of a Russian force hurrying to their aid. The shooting stopped and, very decently, the Koreans moved such transport as they had out of the way.

Perhaps we even waved to each other! Meanwhile I drew my revolver with somewhat of a clammy hand and, of all things, looked at my watch. I therefore know that it took exactly 17 very long minutes for me to review that North Korean brigade.

'However, the files on each side of the road presently thinned out to a trickle of stragglers, and then we were alone again. Our immediate danger now was that we should, in what was now gathering dusk, run into the leading American troops who could well prove more lethal than the North Koreans. Fortunately we came, almost at once, on a track leading off the road and up that we turned, abandoning our vehicles and taking to the bushes. Presently we heard the leading Americans grinding up the road to stop a few hundred yards short of us, but we made no attempt to contact them until morning and daylight. Then we turned about and made our way back to Sariwon. It was not an experience I would wish to repeat. In fact none of us ever spoke about it subsequently. We thought it would be unlucky to do so. As a postscript, our 3in mortar platoon had a little adventure of their own although I only know of it by hearsay. Withdrawing through Sariwon from the positions they had been holding in support of C Coy at the north end of the town, they too found themselves in the company of a large detachment of North Koreans. The disparity in numbers dictated discretion and when the latter addressed the internationally hatted Jocks — they were wearing their woollen cap comforters — as ''Russky'', it was thought as well to maintain the deception for the moment. An entente was established, cigarettes and unintelligible conversation was exchanged, and Lt Fairrie, the platoon commander, had a North Korean ''comfort girl'' issued to him. She immediately got in his jeep and further cemented relations by exchanging hats with him. It was however, a situation with no future and it ended, as it had to, with an exchange of shots as a result of which the Koreans made off and Fairrie lost his ''comfort girl''.* He did, however, manage to retrieve his balmoral.'

Thus ended one of the strangest days that the Argylls spent in Korea and one that none of them were likely to forget in a hurry!

* The *Saturday Evening Post* reporter when describing the action, attributed its sudden ending to a stray American, who came on the scene without knowing what was going on. When addressed as 'Russky?' he replied, 'Hell, no!' — and that was when all the shooting started!

Helicopters in Korea

Casevac

During World War 2 aircraft were occasionally used by both sides to move sick and wounded to places of medical care and hospitalisation but this was always considered as an emergency method to be used only when casualties could not be transported by normal means, such as stretcher bearer, ambulance, hospital train or ship. The Korean War dramatically changed all that. Casualty evacuation by helicopter direct from the front line became the latest and most successful method in the medical evacuation chain. Flight surgeons and medical technicians of the US Air Rescue Service also introduced new inflight techniques to save life, such as blood transfusions, which were completed before the patient's arrival at the MASH (Mobile Army Surgical Hospital). Undoubtedly, however, it was the speed and absence of jolting over rough terrain that really saved lives. Out of every 1,000 wounded men who reached hospital in WW2, an average of 45 subsequently died of their wounds, while in Korea only 25 out of every 1,000 were lost. The Air Rescue Service alone evacuated over 10,000 wounded in Korea, and as a satisfied 'customer' I can personally vouch for their speed and efficiency. Fixed wing aircraft were also used to transport the wounded back to base hospitals in Japan, and subsequently back home if that proved necessary. But it was the helicopter which was the real lifesaver. The casevac chopper, with its immediately recognisable external pods (containing stretchers), became a regular sight in the battle area. It was estimated that they could normally get a casualty on to an operating table within an hour of his being wounded,

Other roles

Evacuation was of course not the only use of the helicopter, with other tasks being liaison, courier, reconnaissance and transport. The US Army and US Air Force initially had various 'agreements' about the use by the Army of aircraft, such as those needed for artillery spotting, local liaison and courier duty, these agreements limiting the size, weight and range of such aircraft. They also covered those aircraft needed for improving and expediting ground combat and logistics within the combat zone (ie the area from the frontline rearwards for some 60 to 75 miles). These agreements also stipulated that while the Air Force had a primary function to provide airlift to the Army, Army aircraft would also transport supplies, equipment and small units within the combat zone. In the autumn of 1951 Gen Ridgway was so impressed by the value of the US Marine helicopters in Korea, that he asked the Department of the Army to provide four helicopter transport battalions, each of 280 helicopters. Although the war had entered its last stages before either the Army or the Air Force began to receive significant numbers of transport helicopters, their value for the future was expressed thus by Gen Maxwell D. Taylor, who took over the Eighth Army from Gen Van Fleet in May 1952, when he said: 'The cargo helicopter, employed en masse, can extend the tactical mobility of the Army far beyond its normal capability. I hope that the United States Army will make ample provisions for the full exploitation of the helicopter in the future.'

Below: Three-star helicopter belonging to the Corps Commander arriving at the 1 DWR heli-pad.
Maj L. Kershaw

Above: Christmas dinner by helicopter! An outpost of 3rd Infantry Division receives its Christmas dinner in a novel manner, 25 December 1952. *US Army*

Right: Another important helicopter used in Korea was the Sikorsky H-19. Given the name Chickasaw (in line with the US Army practice of allocating Indian tribal names to its helicopters) it was first obtained for the US Army in 1952, 72 H-19Cs and 336 H-190s being ordered. Here an H-19 lifts engineer stores on an Australian position. *Australian War Memorial*

The Chinese attack

The Chinese Communist Forces

As the UN forces moved closer to the Yalu River in the autumn of 1950, about 300,000 Chinese Peoples Volunteers, mainly comprising units from the 4th Field Army, lay in wait for them. On 26 November, the commander of the Chinese 'volunteers', Gen Lin Pao, sprang the trap and launched his forces against the American and South Koreans. The main weight of the attack was in the centre against the ROK II Corps. There followed in the next two months, the longest retreat in US military history. The elements of the Chinese People's Liberation Army (PLA) which entered Korea were normally referred to as the Chinese Communist Forces (CCF) in official documents. In the press they were pictured in those early days as 'drug crazed fanatics', who attacked in screaming hordes and relied on 'human wave' tactics to overcome the opposition, regardless of casualties. Nothing could have actually been further from the truth. A more realistic appraisal appeared in the US Marine Corps history of the Korean War:

'Although the Chinese Reds were represented by a peasant army, it was also a first-rate army when judged by its own tactical and strategic standards. Military poverty might be blamed for some of its deficiencies in arms and equipment, but its semi-guerilla tactics were based on a mobility which could not be burdened with heavy weapons and transport. The Chinese coolie in the padded cotton uniform could do one thing better than any other soldier on earth; he could infiltrate around an enemy position in the darkness with unbelievable stealth. Only Americans who have had such an experience can realise

Below: Men at a mortar observation post belonging to Company A, 17th Infantry Regiment, 7th US Infantry Division, keep an alert watch for the enemy. *US Army*

Above: Men of an infantry company under attack.
US Army

Right: An infantryman engages the enemy with his .30 carbine. *US Army*

what a shock it is to be surprised at midnight with the grenades and submachine gun slugs of gnomelike attackers who seem to rise out of the very earth. Press correspondents were fond of referring to the "human sea tactics of the Asiatic hordes". Nothing could be further from the truth. In reality, the Chinese seldom attacked in units larger than a regiment. Even these efforts were usually reduced by a seemingly endless succession of platoon infiltrations. It was not mass but deception and surprise which made the Chinese Reds formidable... A generation of warfare against material odds had established a pattern of attack which proved effective against armies possessing an advantage in arms and equipment. One Marine officer aptly described a Chinese attack as "assembly on the objective". The coolie in the CCF ranks had no superior in the world at making long approach marches by night, hiding by day, with as many as fifty men sharing a hut or cave and subsisting on a few handfuls of rice apiece. Night attacks were so much the rule that an exception came as a surprise. The advancing columns took such natural routes as draws and stream beds, deploying as soon as they met resistance. Combat groups then peeled off from the tactical columns, one at a

Above: A platoon leader hurls a hand grenade at the enemy.
US Army

time, and closed with rifles, submachine guns and grenades. Once engaged and under fire, the attackers hit the ground. Rising at any lull, they came on until engaged again; but when fully committed, they did not relinquish the attack even when riddled with casualties. Other Chinese came forward to take their places, and the build-up continued until a penetration was made, usually on the front of one or two platoons. After consolidating the ground, the combat troops then crept or wriggled forward against the open flank of the next platoon position. Each step of the assault was executed with practised stealth and boldness, and the results of several such penetrations on a battalion front could be devastating. The pattern of attack was varied somewhat to suit different occasions.

'CCF attacking forces range as rule from a platoon to a company in size, being continually built up as casualties thinned the ranks . . . After giving CCF tactics due credit for their merits, some serious weaknesses were also apparent. The primitive logistical system put such restrictions on ammunition supplies, particularly artillery and mortar shells, that a Chinese battalion sometimes had to be pulled back to wait for replenishment if the first night's

attack failed. At best the infantry received little help from supporting arms. POW interrogation revealed that in many instances each soldier was issued with 80 rounds of small arms ammunition upon crossing the Yalu. This was his total supply. The artillery and mortars were so limited that they must reserve fire for the front line, passing up lucrative targets in the rear areas. Some attempts were made to bring up reserve stocks to forward supply dumps about 30 miles behind the front, but not much could be accomplished with animal and human transport.* A primitive communications system also accounted for CCF short-comings. The radio net only extended down to regimental level, and telephones only to battalions and occasionally companies. Below battalion, communications depended upon runners or such signalling devices as bugles, whistles, flares and flashlights. The consequence of this was tactical rigidity which at times was fatal. Apparently CCF commanding officers had little or no option below battalion level. A battalion once committed to the attack often kept on as long as its ammunition lasted, even if events indicated that it was beating its brains out against the strongest part of the opposing line. The result in many instances was tactical suicide. After these defects are taken into full account, however, the Chinese soldier and the Korean terrain made a fomidable combination. Ironically, Americans fighting the first war of the new Atomic Age were encountering conditions reminiscent of the border warfare waged by their pioneer forefathers against the Indians.'

Artillery at Kunu-ri
Undoubtedly the most worrying time of the war for the United Nations Command was when the CCF joined the battle. Cock-a-hoop at the trouncing that they were giving the North Koreans, lulled into a false sense of security by rumours that the war was as good as over and that they would all be 'Home for Christmas', the men of the Eighth Army were taken completely

* As someone who has suffered under a heavy Chinese bombardment during the Third Battle of the Hook in May 1953, I cannot entirely support this comment. Certainly, when they needed to, the CCF could produce plenty of shells to support an attack and to maintain the weight of this support, if they considered the position a tough one to crack. The figures for incoming rounds on to the Hook position amounted to over 20,000 rounds of mixed shells and mortar bombs over a 10-day period, with at least half (ie 10,000 mixed shells and mortar bombs) falling on to 1 DWR positions on the night of the main attack 28/29 May — so much for a supposed lack of ammunition!

unawares. A fighting withdrawal is probably the most difficult operation of war to carry out successfully, it can so easily turn into a rout, especially when the enemy is able to infiltrate in strength behind and in between the forward localities, to set up roadblocks, ambushes, etc on routes by which the withdrawal is taking place. In such circumstances, all the modern paraphernalia of war, especially road bound transport, becomes more of a hindrance than a help. The need is to be able to move rapidly, but to retain order and cohesion, not allowing the enemy to gain the initiative. But it is very easy to say and particularly difficult to achieve! The following story shows just a fraction of the difficulties and dangers that beset the UN ground forces as they beat an undignified retreat in front of the CCF. It concerns the US 17th Field Artillery Battalion who were equipped with 8in howitzers, and is taken from *Combat Actions in Korea*. The battalion was attached to the 2nd Infantry Division on 24 November 1950, after being relieved from control of the 1st Cavalry Division. They moved into positions in the vicinity of Kujang-dong, ready to cover, not a final victorious move to the frontier, but rather, as the Americans tactical doctrine puts it, 'a displacement to the rear' (ie a withdrawal/retreat) in front of the massive Chinese assault. Kujang-dong was not much of a town, a few dozen mud-coloured houses bordering a narrow road and a single track railway. A Battery put its guns at the edge of the village and took over some of the better buildings for sleeping quarters and their command post. The action which followed gives a graphic picture of the hardfought withdrawal in bitter weather:

'At this time Battery A had a strength of 74 of the 135 authorised men, having come overseas understrength in August. Soon after the battery arrived in Korea, 50 ROK soldiers were sent to Battery A and had stayed until October, when they had been released because everyone thought the war was over. The first indication Battery A had that the war wasn't over came on the morning of 24 November from an air observer, who, while registering the No 2 howitzer on the base point, spotted an estimated 200 enemy soldiers. It had been a month or more since anyone had seen so many North Koreans, and no one realised that these soldiers were Chinese. The front line was not more than 3,000 yards north of Kujang-dong when Battery A began firing. Expecting to continue the usual rapid northward advance, the battalion commander (Lt-Col Elmer H. Harrelson) went forward on the morning of 25 Nov-

ember to select positions two miles further north. At the same time the commander of the nearby 61st Field Artillery Battalion (a 105mm unit) selected positions in the same area. Both units were to move that afternoon, but the road was already so jammed with traffic, that Division Artillery decided not to move the 8in howitzers until the next morning. Early that night Chinese troops waded the Chongchon River and attacked in force, hitting units of the 23rd Infantry Regiment and overrunning the new positions of the 61st Field Artillery Regiment. At 2300 some of the men from the 61st straggled into the area of Battery A, having left their position with neither equipment nor howitzers. One man was barefoot. The commander of Battery A (Capt Allen L. Myers) put everyone on an alert basis for the night, although the Chinese did not penetrate that far.

'After daybreak, 26 November, the commanding general of the 2nd Infantry Division Artillery ordered Col Harrelson to pull back several miles. While the 61st Battalion attacked to recover its howitzers and equipment, Harrelson selected positions to the rear. The narrow supply road was still so jammed with vehicles, however, that it was late that night before Battery A received the march order, and it was 2330 before the battery pulled on to the road and started south, moving under blackout conditions. The chief of section of the last howitzer in the column put his hand on the shoulder of the man driving the tractor to indicate that he wanted the driver to slow down through the town of Kujang-dong. The driver, thinking that the section chief wanted him to turn left, turned down a small side street. There was a delay of five or ten minutes while the crew turned the tractor and howitzer around, knocking down several small buildings in the process. This section was now separated from the rest of the column and it was impossible to catch up because of the solid line of vehicles, but Capt Myers had taken his section chiefs with him when he selected the new position and the men knew where to go.

'Capt Myer's new position was in a stream bed near the road to Kunu-ri. Three howitzer sections arrived first; then the maintenance, wire, kitchen and radio sections; then the fourth gun section; and finally the local security detail. The temperature was near zero and there was a strong wind as the crews put the guns into firing positions. Battery A fired without registering, using average corrections furnished by the fire direction centre. On 27 November, while the infantry regiments of the 2nd Division and some of the artillery units were experiencing heavy enemy attacks, Battery A had a comparatively quiet day, although it was too cold for the men to sleep. They sat huddled around gasoline stoves when they had no fire missions. All men whom Capt Myers could spare from the firing sections were needed for outpost duty or for hauling ammunition from Kunu-ri. The narrow road, following the curves of the Chongchon River, was better suited to the native ox-carts than the heavy trucks that now jammed it, moving only a few miles an hour. Enemy pressure increased throughout the division's area and at 2200 that night, Col Harrelson received orders to displace to the rear. By 0745 the following morning 28 November, when Battery A march-ordered, front line infantry units had fallen back until the artillerymen could hear the sound of small arms fire. Capt Myers heard that an ROK division west of the 2nd Infantry Division, had collapsed, exposing the division's right flank. This time Myers moved his battery approximately five miles south, where he put the howitzers in a new position near the road, but at 1230, with the battery laid and ready to fire in the new position, he was ordered to close station and march-order, again moving south. By this time all units

of 2nd Division were moving back. Battery A now went into position south-west of Kunu-ri in a large field along the division's supply road. The first part of the night was quiet and the men had a chance to sleep some, but the battery began getting fire missions and commenced shooting in a northerly direction two hours before daylight, 29 November.

'Several incidents occurred during the day that indicated the situation was fast becoming critical. Early in the morning Col Harrelson received instructions to look for new positions along the route of withdrawal to Sunchon. Earlier, however, a report reached HQ 2nd Division indicating that the enemy had established a roadblock several miles south on the road to Sunchon. Officers at the division's command post accepted this information calmly, but sent a patrol to investigate and, a little later that morning, ordered the Reconnaissance Company out to open the road. Meanwhile, the reconnaissance for new positions was held up until afternoon when, as officers at division expected, the Reconnaissance Company would have eliminated the enemy roadblock on the Kunu-ri-Sunchon road. About mid-morning, Capt Myers received orders to haul the ammunition he needed from

Below: Typical task for combat engineers was road repair work, such as this carried out by Company B, 13th Combat Engineer Battalion, 7th Infantry Division, south of Paegchpo-ri, 13 March 1951. *US Army*

Kunu-ri because the ammunition dump there was going to be destroyed. And during the day the three 105mm howitzer battalions and the 155mm howitzer battery of the 2nd Division passed by the gun positions of Battery A, all headed south. Col Harrelson, Capt Myers and the other battery commanders, undertook that afternoon to reconnoitre for positions on the Sunchon road, expecting it to be open. It wasn't. Vehicles were jammed on and near the road for several miles south of Kunu-ri, and occupants of some vehicles returning from the south claimed the road was cut, and that it was impossible to get through. Capt Myers and his party returned to the battery position at dark while Col Harrelson went to Division's Artillery CP for a briefing on the general situation. There he learned the 2nd Division was confident it would be able to open the road. He was told to fire his regular missions during the night. If the road were open by morning of 30 November, the 17th Field Artillery Battalion would withdraw over the road, taking its place at the head of the column of artillery battalions, since the 8in howitzers were considered to be the most valuable pieces and the hardest to replace. If the roadblock were not cleared by morning — and if division did not issue another order — the battalion was to pull out by another road west of Anju and then south toward Pyongyang. Col Harrelson received this information between 2200 and 2300. Since the division's command post was being attacked at that time, he realised that the situation could change abruptly.

'The direction of fire, which was north on the morning of 29 November, gradually shifted east during the day. That evening, with the howitzers laid on the azimuth of 1,600 mils, Battery A started firing charge 7 at a range of 18,000 yards. By the morning of 30 November the cannoneers were using charge 1 at a range of 1,300 yards. Because of the critical situation Col Harrelson, calm but anxious to keep the battery informed, held three battery commanders' calls during the night. At the call held at 0400 on 30 November he outlined three possible plans of action: to return to Kunu-ri and put a large ammunition trailer across the road to block the traffic long enough to get the battalion's vehicles into the solid column of traffic and move the battalion west through Anju; to go south on the 2nd Division order when the roadblock was opened; if these failed, he proposed that the battalion stay and fight its way south as a battalion. Harrelson preferred to take the road to Anju since his battalion had followed that road when it moved north and was familiar with it. However, soon after this meeting Col Harrelson was called to the Division Artillery command post and there learned that, by division order, his battalion would withdraw over the road to Sunchon. During the night 29-30 November, the military police told the division's provost marshal that the road to Anju was also cut by the Chinese. At the same time, IX Corps, of which the division was a part, directed the 2nd Division to use the Sunchon road since the road from Anju south was already burdened by three divisions.

'Soldiers continued to straggle through and past Battery A's position during the early morning of 30 November. Some were ROK soldiers and some were from the 2nd Division or from another nearby US division. Soon after daylight a tank officer stopped at Battery A's position and told Capt Myers that all infantry units to the north had withdrawn. He said he had some tanks in the rear that could help the artillerymen if necessary. This was not an accurate report, but, as a precaution, Myers assigned zones for direct fire to each of the gun sections. Even as the situation was, the cannoneers could see the shell bursts from their gun positions. Col Harrelson met his battery commanders

Below: Two demolition men of the 2nd Engineer Battalion, 2nd US Infantry Division, deactivate one of several mines found in Mundal, January 1951. The mines are probably captured US M-6 anti-tank mines. *US Army*

Above: Men of 13th Combat Engineer Battalion, 7th Infantry Division, construct a treadway bridge across the Choyang River, 10 April 1951. *US Army*

Top right: An anti-tank crew prodding for enemy mines after the M4A3 tank belonging to 32 RCT, 7th Infantry Division (in background) has been disabled by a mine on the road just outside Hadewa, 28 February 1951. Visible at right is the damaged track. *US Army*

Bottom right: M4A3 tanks of 32nd Infantry Regiment, cover men of Company L, 32 RCT, 7th Infantry Division, as they advance down the road to Chae-jae, 1 March 1951. By now UN forces were slowing down in the face of stiff enemy opposition. *US Army*

again at 0800 on 30 November and told them of the decision to use the road to Sunchon even though the road leading west to Anju still appeared open. The 2nd Division, he said, had ordered the 9th Infantry Regiment to attack south and destroy the enemy roadblock. The 9th Infantry, however, had suffered such heavy casualties during the last three days' fighting that it had an attacking force of only 400 or 500 men when it started south toward the critical area early that morning. By 0900 it became apparent at Div HQ that this force was too weak to destroy the roadblock, and the 38th Infantry was ordered to help. At 0930 Col Harrelson called Capt Myers with instructions to march-order and move as a fighting column. Myers first interpreted this to mean he should destroy all equipment, but before he did so, he called his battalion commander again and learned that Col Harrelson wanted the tractors and howitzers to go first, then the wheeled vehicles with the rest of the equipment. He wanted the tops and windshields down, machine guns mounted and the men equipped to fight as infantrymen if necessary. By batteries, the order of march was: B, A, HQ, Service, C. Within Battery A the four gun sections left first; then the tractor pulling the large ammunition trailer, the Diamond-T four ton ammunition truck, and the $\frac{3}{4}$ton executive truck. The rest of the wheeled vehicles followed. Moving south at an average rate of 5mph, Battery A passed three of the 2nd Division's organic artillery battalions — all still in position and firing. It appeared to members of Battery A that the guns were laid to fire in several directions. About noon the column stopped when Battery A's vehicles were near a deserted quarter-

master supply dump that had belonged to the US 25th Infantry Division. Here the men loaded up on quartermaster supplies, especially overcoats, which many of them lacked. Near the supply dump a hundred or more soldiers, American and South Koreans, were lying on the ground trying to sleep. A captain was in charge of them. There was a two-hour delay at the dump, while the remaining fighting force of two infantry regiments attempted to reduce the enemy positions on the roadblock. At about 1400 the column started moving again, and the infantry men by the supply dump climbed up on Battery A's vehicles. Vehicles were closed up bumper to bumper on the dry road which, having been graded by US engineers, was wide enough for two way traffic in most places. Low hills lay on both sides of the 2,000-yard wide valley.

'The day was cold. The men were tired and tense. After proceeding haltingly for a mile and a half or two miles, the battery's vehicles passed between enemy machine guns firing from opposite sides of the road and the men scrambled for the ditches. Friendly airplanes strafed the hills along the road, occasionally quieting the guns. When they did, the column would get under way until another gun fired or until the vehicles ahead came under enemy fire. After passing several enemy machine guns, all located between 200 and 300 yards from the road, the column stopped again and this time failed to move until almost dark. Military police patrolled the road in jeeps, doubling the column to locate the trouble. During the halt a large number of South Korean soldiers came across the enemy-occupied hills on the left side of the road and joined the column. They were badly disorganised and some without weapons. Meanwhile, Col Harrelson,

fearing that his battalion would be stranded in the centre of the roadblock through the night, made plans to pull his vehicles off the road and form a perimeter, but at dusk the vehicles began moving again. About this time a halftrack mounting twin 40mm came past the column and took position at the head of Battery A. It fired at all suspected enemy positions, often getting airbusts by aiming at the trees. Many of the South Korean soldiers climbed on the vehicles as they started moving. After dark drivers used only blackout lights, and it was difficult to distinguish the many vehicles abandoned by the road from other vehicles in the column. The communications chief (Sgt Preston L. Bryson) was driving the executive truck and pulled up behind a jeep in which he could see two men. After waiting several minutes, he realised both men were dead and then pulled around the jeep. There were 25 to 30 vehicles abandoned along the seven-mile stretch that was under enemy fire.

'The main difficulty occurred at the southern end of the roadblock. A two-lane concrete bridge had been destroyed, forcing the withdrawing column to use a bypass and to ford the stream which, at the time, was several feet deep. The bypass approach from the north was in good condition, but the southern exit was up terraced rice paddies, the first terrace being very difficult to manoeuvre. After fording the stream, the driver of the first tractor in Capt Myer's column found his path blocked by two $\frac{3}{4}$ton trucks and one $2\frac{1}{2}$ton truck that were stuck and abandoned. None of the abandoned vehicles belonged to the 17th Artillery Battalion. The battalion S3 (Maj Joseph J. Prusaitis) came back and instructed Capt Myers to uncouple the first tractor and pull the vehicles out of the bypass. The lead tractor belonged to the 2nd Section (Sgt Harrington D. Hawkins) which uncoupled just as two tanks drove up the road from the south with their lights on. The beams of the headlights fell on the men working in the bypass. Immediately several enemy machine guns opened fire and tracer bullets flashed all around the artillerymen. Mortar rounds began falling nearby. The battery executive (Lt Donal D. Judd) was standing on the road when the lights shone on him. A Chinese rifleman 30ft away was aiming at Judd when one of his cannoneers killed the enemy soldier. After this action flared up the tanks turned off their lights and began firing at the enemy. Thinking that the tanks had come to pull the abandoned vehicles away, Capt Myers instructed Sgt Hawkins to couple up again and proceed. Meanwhile, on the north side of the destroyed bridge, M/Sgt Judge Shanks, driving the next howitzer, looked across and saw the tank on the south side of the bridge. Not realising there was a gap in the bridge, he pulled on the north approach when he was forced to halt. The following vehicle stopped a few feet behind him and the rest of the column was jammed up to the rear. This caused another difficult delay before the 8-inch howitzer and prime mover could be backed up and run through the bypass.

'The bypass was the end of the roadblock. At 2130 the last of the men of Battery A cleared the obstacle and saw the lights come at the head of the column. There were stragglers and wounded men on the trailers, howitzers, fenders and hoods of the vehicles, and three ¾ton trucks

had been turned into ambulances. The artillerymen had passed the bodies of at least 400 American and other friendly troops that were lying by the road. Battery A had eight men wounded while running the roadblock, none killed. It lost four 2½ton trucks, three ¾ton trucks, the kitchen trailer and the supply trucks of which one was abandoned because of mechanical failure. For the battalion the equipment losses amounted to 26 vehicles and a howitzer from Battery B, which overturned and killed eight ROK soldiers who were riding on it. The artillery battalions and other units of the 2nd Division that followed were not so fortunate. Soon after Col Harrelson's battalion cleared the bypass, an M6 tractor pulling a 155mm howitzer stalled in the middle of the ford, effectively blocking the route of withdrawal. All vehicles north of the ford were abandoned and the personnel walked out.'

The withdrawal continued until the last week of December, when the Eighth Army managed to stabilise the situation temporarily along the line of the 38th Parallel, but they were unable to hold the enemy for long. Crossing the frontier, the Reds took Seoul in early January 1951 and continued to push southwards. The UN forces tried again unsuccessfully to hold up the enemy behind the Han River, and had to give more ground. However, by mid-January, it was clear that the main impetus of the attack was over, the front was stabilised and almost at once the UN forces took the initiative and attacked. Seoul was recaptured in mid-March and by 8 April the front was again stabilised along the 38th Parallel. But the respite was only to be a temporary one.

It was of course during the winter withdrawal that the Eighth Army lost their gallant commander Gen 'Johnny' Walker. On the day the last UN troops fell back across the 38th Parallel (23 December), he was killed when his jeep skidded on an icy road while travelling at high speed. His place was taken by Lt-Gen Matthew B. Ridgway, one of the United States most courageous commanders of World War 2, who was flown from USA to replace him. Gen Ridgway was another no nonsense commander, with a tremendous personality, which he put to good effect to revitalise the flagging spirits of UN forces. He was known, somewhat irreverently by the troops a 'Old Iron-Tits', because of his penchant for wearing primed hand grenades, dangling from his top pockets, but these, like Gen George Patton's ivory handled six shooters, were merely an eye-catching gimmick.

Below: With 'A' frames strapped to their backs, Korean labourers carry supplies to men of the 65th RCT, 3rd Infantry Division, 21 March 1951. *US Army*

Presidential Citations

In Korea, as in every other modern war, outstanding acts of bravery on the battlefield were acknowledged by the presentation of decorations to the individuals concerned, not only by their own country, but also on some occasions by others, especially by the Republic of Korea and the United States of America. Awards were also given to entire units as well as to individuals, and one of the most prized was the Distinguished Unit Citation awarded by the President of the United States of America. As we shall see in this chapter, British and Commonwealth units were awarded this coveted honour, but they were not alone. Other units of the UN forces also had their acts of bravery recognised in this unique way. Unfortunately, I do not have enough space to cover them all, so here are but two examples. They are the awards made to the French and Netherlands battalions during January-February 1951, while they were both serving as part of the US 2nd Infantry (Indian Head) Division.

The citation for the French battalion explains how they displayed extraordinary heroism while in action in the vicinity of Chipyong-ni, during the period 30 January to February 1951. Advancing as part of the 23rd Regimental Combat Team, with the mission of locating and engaging the 42nd Chinese Army whose positions were not known, the French battalion, together with an American infantry battalion supported by artillery and tanks, began to attack up the Kumdang Chon Valley at 0900 on 31 January. The attack progressed very slowly over the rugged and mountainous terrain, until the French battalion, on the left, seized Hill 453, a critical feature which not only dominated the area to the south, but also overlooked a northern valley divided by two ridges through

Below: Men of the French Battalion, armed with an American portable M2-2 flamethrower. *ECP Armees*

which two railway tunnels ran on an east-west axis. With the French on this hill, the rest of the objective was easily taken by 1815 hours and the force immediately began to occupy and organise the defence of the high ground around the tunnels. One French company was placed on Hill 453, and the rest of the battalion deployed on the ridges to the north, making up the western half of the perimeter. At 0600 on the morning of 1 February, after the US battalion on the eastern half of the perimeter had been under attack for over an hour, the French were heavily attacked by the 373rd Chinese Infantry Regiment. By 1020, this regiment had employed its full strength against the French battalion and had reached the crest of Hill 453. The French company on the hill counter-attacked with the bayonet and drove the enemy back. By noon, elements of another Chinese regiment had gained a high, rocky hill on the north-west corner of the perimeter from which they brought direct machine gun fire down on to the area of the French CP. The French 3rd Company, deploying along the crest, attacked this lodgement under cover of recoilless rifle and tank fire, drove the enemy off and restored the lines. The crisis came in the early afternoon, with the French 1st and 3rd Companies still under heavy attack and with no air support available due to ground fog which covered the entire area all morning. However, it finally lifted and 24 aircraft sorties were brought in, and observed mortar and artillery fire placed on the masses of attacking enemy. Under this fire, the enemy broke off and withdrew at 1800 hours, just as a relief American battalion arrived from the south. The next day, 1,300 dead Chinese soldiers were actually counted in front of the

perimeter, the majority being found in front of the French battalion's positions. Of the 225 casualties suffered by the task force, 125 were French. As a result of their bravery, the positions were held and the 373rd Chinese Infantry Regiment was routed.

The Netherlands battalion was awarded their Presidential Citation for heroism in combat at Hoengsong and Wonju, during the period 12-15 February 1951. On the early morning of 12 February, the enemy launched an offensive with two divisions, aimed at splitting the central front. Against this onslaught the Netherlands battalion had the mission of maintaining blocking positions on the outskirts of the important communications centre at Hoengsong, with the aim of enabling two American battalions, supporting artillery and the remnants of the 5th and 8th ROK Divisions, to withdraw from their exposed positions where they were now surrounded. The Dutch soldiers were deployed astride the main enemy axis of advance. Large groups of enemy approached along the high ground to the west and on the ridges to the north. A small group penetrated the Dutch positions but was quickly repulsed. All that afternoon, the Netherlands battalion covered the withdrawal of the other UN forces. After darkness had fallen, a company of enemy managed to infiltrate with the withdrawing ROK troops.

They succeeded in passing around the open flank of the Dutch positions and reached the area of the command post. Recognising the enemy, the Netherlands commander shouted a warning to his troops, and, rallying his headquarters personnel, led them against the enemy until he was mortally wounded. His gallant example so inspired his staff, they they

Right: Dutch soldiers in action in Korea.
Royal Netherlands Embassy

Below right: A Dutch soldier behind his water cooled Browning .30 machine gun, the standard support MG.
Royal Netherlands Army

repelled the enemy, killing many of them in fierce hand-to-hand combat. The battered and courageous Dutch troops then withdrew to successive blocking positions, until they had covered the last of the friendly forces as they broke through the enemy lines. They had fought against enormous odds and gained the precious time necessary for the friendly forces to get clear. Digging in on 13 February, the Dutch waited for the next onslaught which duly arrived against B Company early the following morning. The company was forced back until mortar and artillery fire could be brought to bear on the enemy. By the evening of the 14th the situation was critical. The enemy were now in full control of Hill 325, a dominant feature which overlooked their positions. Communications were broken and the situation 'fluid'. At the time A Company, which was so understrength that it had to be reinforced by platoons from both B Company and the Heavy Mortar Company, was ordered to retake the hill. Launching their first counter-attack at 0230 hours 15 February, they were beaten back by heavy machine gun fire from the top of the hill. They tried again at 0345. This time they got within 300 yards of the crest, before being repulsed for a second time. At 0600 hours, after two setbacks and three sleepless nights of fighting, short of ammunition and out of communications, they snatched victory from defeat by fixing bayonets and storming the hill. Shouting their famous *Van Heutz* battle cry, they slashed their way to the crest of the hill through the last remaining enemy.

The Chinese spring offensive

The early days of April 1951 saw the Eighth Army continuing its advance northwards, with the aim of securing a line of commanding ground north of the 38th Parallel. It had been known for some time, however, that the Chinese were preparing yet another large scale offensive to check the UN advance and to drive them southwards again. This attack was launched on 22 April and in the desperate battles that followed, both the 27th Commonwealth Infantry Brigade and the British 29th Infantry Brigade, gained imperishable glory. 29 Brigade was operating under US I Corps, holding the line of the Imjin River about 35 miles due north of Seoul, while 27 Brigade, under US IX Corps and in support of the ROK 6th Division, was in the Kapyong River area, about 35 miles north-east of Seoul. Dealing chronologically with the two actions, 29 Brigade was the first to feel the full weight of the Chinese attack, so I will cover their battle first.

The Glorious Glosters

'The battle honour Imjin is one of 36 carried on the Regimental Colour of the 1st Battalion the Gloucestershire Regiment. All are remembered with pride, but IMJIN like EGYPT, has brought a distinctive badge of honour. The latter records the gallant action of the 28th Foot at the Battle of Alexandria, 21 March 1801, when fighting back to back, the soldiers of the 28th repulsed the attacks of the French. Subsequently the 28th were granted the distinction of wearing their regimental number on the back of their head-dress, in addition to their front badge. 150 years later at IMJIN the successors to the old 28th Foot were to fight for three days and nights completely surrounded and were to earn another unique distinction for the Regiment — the United States Presidential Distinguished Unit Citation. Its insignia, a blue streamer inscribed SOLMA-RI, is carried on the pike of the Regimental Colour.'*

*Taken from the introduction to the *Imjin Roll* by Col E. D. Harding DSO and published here by kind permission of the author and RHQ, The Gloucestershire Regiment.

On 13 April 1951, Gen Peng Teh-Huai, Supreme Commander of the 1st Chinese Communist Forces Field Army, gave out orders to begin a fresh offensive and sent small reconnaissance parties to infiltrate the UN lines to the south and report on their dispositions. The aim of this major offensive was to be the capture of Seoul and the cutting off and destruction of all the UN forces to the east of the capital. At the time the British 29th Independent Infantry Brigade Group, under Brig Tom Brodie, had moved up from I Corps reserve to take over positions along the line of the Imjin River on a nine-mile front. The brigade then consisted of four infantry battalions — 1 Royal Northumberland Fusiliers, 1 Glosters, 1 Royal Ulster Rifles and the Belgian Battalion (attached). There were two vital defiles to be covered through the jagged razor-backed hills,

Below: The Glosters battle, 22-25 April 1951.

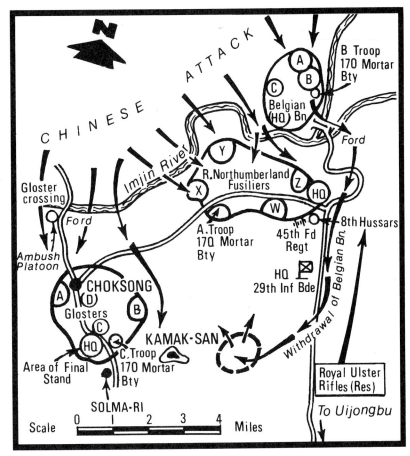

75

which offered the Chinese the fastest means of reaching the good going some miles to the south. The dispositions of the brigade are illustrated with the Belgian battalion on the high ground just north of the Imjin River and close to its junction with the Han River. 1 RNF were in the centre, with the Glosters on their left, covering the main track which led south from the river. The Ulsters were in reserve. On the left of the brigade was the ROK 1st Division, with responsibility for the ground running to the coast. The Glosters position covered one of the classic invasion routes to the south and the one which would be used by the crack 63rd Chinese Army (composed of three divisions, 187, 188 and 189, each of about 9,000 men) which was poised to spearhead the main assault. Speed was the essence of the Chinese plan, a rapid night march to the river followed by the destruction of the UN forces covering it, and then further speedy exploitation to the south. Gen Peng Teh-Huai was confident that his forces would reach Seoul within 36 hours, as they began to move towards the river on the evening of 21 April.

Col James Power Carne, who was commanding the Glosters, was faced with the normal dilemma which most COs face in a defensive position; namely too much ground to cover with too few troops. This was in fact the same problem facing the brigadier and just as there were large gaps between battalion positions, so also had the Gloster companies to be dispersed. There was also a shortage of defence stores, such as wire and mines, so company locations

were not as strong as Col Carne would have liked. A Company, under Maj Pat Angier, was the left forward company, holding the Castle Hill feature, just west of Choksong, and covering the main crossing point on the river some 2,000 yards to the north. To the south-east 1,500 yards away, D Company commanded by Capt Mike Harvey (his company commander was on leave in Japan) held Point 182, while further to the east, B Company, under the Maj Denis Harding, guarded the right flank and the two-mile gap between the Glosters and the next battalion. In reserve was C Company, under Maj Charles Mitchell, sited on a long, narrow ridge which overlooked the river bed in which Battalion HQ, the battalion mortars and those of C Troop 170 Mortar Battery RA were deployed. Left flank protection was provided by the Assault Pioneer Platoon on Hill 235 west of the track. Forward Observation Officers (FOOs) of 70 Field Battery RA were deployed with the forward companies, while their regiment (45 Field) was in direct support.

This then is the outline setting for the battle in which the battalion would fight nonstop for 72 hours, surrounded, suffering heavy casualties, and from which it would emerge with a new name — *The Glorious Glosters*. To illustrate the action I have been kindly allowed to quote from the privately published *Imjin Roll* by Col E. D. Harding DSO:

'Sunday 22 April dawned a clear, crisp day after a heavy overnight frost. All was quiet along the Brigade front. The Chaplain, Padre Davies, held morning service at the Fusiliers' HQ to mark St George's Day, and then returned to visit his own flock. At A Company he gave communion to two young officers — Curtis and Walters. Both these men were to receive the highest awards for bravery. As the morning passed, reports started to come in of large scale enemy movement north of the river. This advance said much for the toughness of the Chinese soldiers. Facing them was an approach march of some 20 miles, in full battle kit and carrying seven days' ration — sausage shape bandoliers containing soya bean flour. This to be followed by a night attack, and, if successful another march through the hills to establish themselves deep behind the UN positions. During the afternoon the battalion prepared itself for battle. Extra ammunition was brought up from A Echelon and in the company positions weapons were cleaned and defensive fire tasks checked and registered. To ensure early warning of the enemy's approach, a patrol from C Company under Lt Temple was placed at the crossing over the river at dusk. In addition, a listening post from B Company was in position some 1,000 yards to the east. All companies were at 50% stand to.'

Another listening post had been sent out to Gloster Crossing the night before (21/22 April). This was manned by Cpl George Cook, Pte 'Scouse' Hunter and Drummer Anthony Eagles, who were part of Battalion HQ Defence Platoon. They were taken to A Company forward positions by truck and then walked down to the river bank, to a point overlooking what is now called 'Gloster Crossing'. Their position was in part of a very long slit trench, about 4ft deep, and they had a direct telephone link back to the CO and adjutant (Capt A. Farrar-Hockley) at Battalion HQ. They were to stay there all night and this is how Anthony Eagles remembers the night's vigil:

'The three of us settled down for a long wait. It was a nice clear night and gave us a good field of observation for about a half a mile east and west. We had decided that we would have two on observation and the other would sit with the phone, changing round each hour. Sometime within the next three hours, perhaps at about 2200, I whispered to Scouse that I thought I saw movement on the other side of the river. He alerted George Cook who reported back to the adjutant. After a while we could discern 14 figures that, by virtue of their khaki uniforms and rice bags slung like bandoliers, could only be Chinese troops. Suddenly the sky was lit up as the Royal Artillery sent up floating flares requested by the adjutant. We could see the others quite clearly as they reached the point opposite us. The adjutant told Cpl Cook that they must not be allowed to cross. Scouse and I decided we would let them get about half way over and then fire. If they succeeded in getting across, we would use our grenades. When they were in exactly the right position, the two of us opened up with rapid fire. We had a rifle, 50 rounds and two grenades each, but so quickly did we let go at them, that the adjutant asked Cpl Cook who had the Bren gun! "It's Eagles and Hunter with rifles only sir" he replied. We succeeded in killing three of them and their bodies floated down the river. We had apparently wounded four others, as their comrades carried them hurriedly back to the north side and into cover. There was no further action by us, but I can assure you that for the rest of the night we were on a knife edge, as we waited for some form of retaliation. . .

Clearly the party that the listening post had dealt with must have been an advanced recce element, because dusk air sorties on the 22nd reported that there were no major bodies of enemy closer than 10 miles from the river. However, the speed at which the Chinese could move was phenomenal and by 2230 the leading elements of 187 Division were being engaged by Lt Temple's patrol on the Imjin and harassed by artillery and mortar fire. Aided by mortar flares, Temple's men took their toll as wave after wave of the enemy waded across the 150-yard wide river, only to be halted by the patrol's fire. Those on the north bank suffered badly from the artillery and mortar fire. The patrol held its position until their ammunition was all but exhausted and they were in danger of being overrun, they were then withdrawn, at midnight, under artillery cover. The *Imjin Roll* continues:

. . . While Temple's platoon was delaying the Chinese, two other battalions of the 187th Division had crossed the river some one and a half miles further to the west and directed their attack on to A Company. Appreciating that valuable time had been lost in crossing the river, the commander of 187 Division was determined to overrun the Glosters and his first objective was Castle Hill. Further to the east, the 188th Division was exploiting the gap between B Company and the Fusiliers. On Castle Hill, 3 Platoon (Lt Waters) held the ridge to the west whilst 2 Platoon (2-Lt Maycock) held the summit. Further to the rear was 3 Platoon (Lt Curtis) and Company HQ with a section of MMG which could cover both forward platoons. Some weeks earlier US Army engineers had constructed a bunker on the reverse slope of 2 Platoon's position. It had been said that it was to be used as an observation post for the Army Commander, Gen Ridgway. This bunker was to be the scene of some exceptionally bitter fighting. By 2200 hours, A, D and B Companies were reporting enemy movement in front of their positions and had called for defensive fire. During the night the main weight of the attack was directed against A and D Companies. A Company in particular was subjected to a series of attacks, being outnumbered by at least six to one. During the night the Chinese battalions infiltrated between the forward platoons and in the early hours of 23 April had established themselves in strength on top of the hill and got a machine gun into the bunker behind Maycock's platoon. In this fighting Maycock was killed and his platoon lost half its men. Maj Angier realised that unless he restored the position A Company would be overrun. Considerable casualties had been inflicted on the Chinese and their dead and dying littered the slopes of the hill. In the half light of dawn hundreds of Chinese could be seen milling around the company position. Angier ordered Lt Curtis to counter-attack the summit of Castle Hill — neutralise the Chinese holding the bunker and restore the forward positions. Covering fire was provided by the MMG section and by the mortars and artillery. Angier moved forward behind Curtis's platoon in order to keep in touch with the attack. The Chinese reacted violently to this attack and Curtis and his men came under heavy fire as they moved up the reverse slope leading to the bunker. Fighting took place at close quarters and Curtis was wounded. He was dragged back by the small "winkle" group he was leading — Cpl Halpin, L Cpl Mairs and Pte Mercer. Cpl Papworth the medical orderly came forward to attend to him. However, Curtis brushed aside his men's pleas to have his wound attended. Telling them to provide covering fire he ran forward on his own with the intention of eliminating the machine gun established in the bunker. The Chinese seemed nonplussed by his individual effort and Curtis managed to throw a grenade into the bunker before he was cut down. He died immediately. [He was awarded the Victoria Cross posthumously for his bravery.] As this was happening Maj Angier himself was killed as was his FOO, Lt Hudson. At this critical moment all could have been lost but the CSM, Harry Gallagher, took control and seeing nothing could be done to restore the position, brought the remnants of the two forward platoons back to the rear platoon position. At 0830 hours A Company, now

only one officer and 53 men strong, pulled back to Gloster Hill (Point 235), the wounded being brought out of action by the Oxford Carriers which had been sent forward to help A Company. The Chinese made no attempt to follow them up, being pinned down by the artillery, mortar and machine gun fire directed against the Castle Hill feature.

'Meanwhile D Company who had also been heavily engaged were ordered back. One of their platoon positions had been overrun but 12 men got away. The men of A and D Company now took up new positions on the ridges running down from Gloster Hill to the west of L of C. Further to the right, B Company were ordered to withdraw to Hill 314 1,500 yards to their rear. B Company had not been engaged as heavily as the other two companies. They had inflicted crushing casualties on Chinese patrols which attempted to take their position but had suffered no casualties themselves. But to their right they could see hundreds of Chinese moving around the flank, heading for the Kamaksan feature. By 1030 B Company had overrun the Chinese patrols on the 314 feature and established themselves on its summit. With A and D Companies redeployed on the eastern slopes of Gloster Hill to the west of the L of C, and with C and B on the high ground to its east, the free passage of the track through the hills to the south was denied to the Chinese. But Col Carne was well aware that both flanks of the battalion's position had been turned. The night's fighting had upset the Chinese timetable and as long as the Glosters held firm they would be denied a quick break through the hills. Throughout the day the FOOs were continually calling for fire support and great havoc was inflicted on the Chinese who were making their way south on either flank. Unfortunately no air support was available. Had it been, the forward companies might have been able to hold their forward positions longer. During the morning of the 23rd, the wounded were evacuated by road and helicopter, but by about noon the Chinese had established blocks on the track to the rear of the battalion just north of the F Echelon area. Fortunately the F Echelon administrative parties had come forward early with food and ammunition. But now no relief or reinforcement could take place without fighting its way forward. Later in the day the brigade commander informed the CO that an attempt would be made to reinforce the Glosters early on the 24th. Should this be unsuccessful, it was vital that Col Carne held his position. There was no question of withdrawal.

'By dusk all companies knew that they could expect to face another night of hard fighting. In the fading light hundreds of Chinese could be seen forming up in the valleys and the sound of Chinese trumpets was heard through the evening gloom. The Chinese 187th Division had received heavy casualties in the first 24 hours of the battle and it was now the turn of the 188th and 189th Divisions to deliver the coup de grace. Against the Glosters position, the main weight of their attack was to be directed against B and C Companies. After dusk the Chinese had moved forward to the lower slopes of the Hill 314 feature and lined up to climb the slopes supported by their machine guns and mortars. By 2230 hours the battle was joined. Fortunately at first, the Chinese attacks against B were disjointed as they seemed uncertain of the exact positions to attack. They were forced to keep to the ridges leading up the slope and could not make much progress. The defensive fire plan had been carefully coordinated and the combined fire of the infantry, mortars and artillery took terrible toll of the Chinese climbing up the slopes. Line after line of Chinese infantrymen were halted in front of the company positions. But this was a battle of attrition. Despite the killing, fresh units of Chinese came forward and by sheer weight of numbers they overran the two top platoons of C Company. Both Maj Mitchell and the CO realised that if the position was lost Battalion HQ and the mortar positions in the river bed would be exposed. Orders were therefore given for Battalion HQ and the mortars to move up on the slopes of Gloster Hill to join A and D Companies together with the remainder of C Company. B Company could not be pulled back in darkness, so they were told by the CO to

Left: Lt Philip Curtis of the Duke of Cornwall's Light Infantry, attached to the Gloucestershire Regiment, was awarded the Victoria Cross (posthumous) for his magnificent gallantry during the counter-attack by his platoon on to Castle Hill on 23 April 1951. *IWM*

Far left, top: A soldier of the Glosters covers two PoWs with his Sten Mk 5 SMG. *IWM*

Far left, centre: Servicing a .303in Vickers machine gun, note the muzzle recoil booster and barrel jacket. This machine gun first entered British Army service in 1912 and was both rugged and reliable. *IWM*

Far left, bottom: Bryan de Grineau's evocative drawing of the last stand of the Glosters. 'Drummie' Buss can be seen in the foreground playing the regimental calls. *The Illustrated London News*

hold their position until daylight when their withdrawal could be covered. B Company continued throughout the night to hold their now isolated position despite increasing attacks by the Chinese. The FOO, Capt Newcombe, continued to call down fire on the Chinese and shells from 45 Field Regiment were being dropped less than 50 yards in front of the company position.

'As dawn broke the MMGs on Gloster Hill joined in and their fire cut through the Chinese massing on the slopes of Hill 314. Soon after 0800 hours the CO ordered B Company to try to break contact and rejoin the remainder of the battalion on Gloster Hill, some 1,500 yards to the west. It was a difficult operation. Lt Costello's 4 Platoon which had taken the main weight of the Chinese attack were in physical contact with the enemy and the Chinese were holding C Company's original position. As B Company pulled back down the steep reverse slope to their new position, the Company was forced to break up into small parties. On reaching the track below they had to run through heavy fire from both flanks while attempting to get through the main valley to the west. Many were forced to break south across the lower slopes of Kamaksan. Only a small party of about 20 strong under Maj Harding were able to fight their way through to D Company. Of the remainder only two men were to be successful in escaping to the south and rejoining the rest of the brigade.'

As the Chinese fought to encircle the Glosters, the rest of the brigade was equally heavily committed and it was soon clear that any relief for the Glosters would have to come from elsewhere. Accordingly, a mixed force of 10 BCT (Philippino infantry) with light tanks, supported by a squadron of the 8th Hussars under Maj Henry Huth, moved up the L of C towards Kwang Suwon, early on the 24th. They reached the F Echelon area successfully, but were eventually halted in the face of increasing Chinese pressure at about 1630, still some four miles south of the Glosters' position. A second attempt by an even stronger force, was planned for the following morning. In the meantime it was essential for the Glosters to stand firm. With less than 50% of his battalion left, many of whom were wounded, low on ammunition and other essentials, Col Carne realised that it would only be possible to survive for another night if they tightened the perimeter drastically. He therefore made plans to move everyone up to the top of Gloster Hill, from where they could still dominate the northern entrance to the

track through the hills and deny the Chinese free access. The southern and western slopes of the hill were precipitous and the northern edges steep, so the only avenues of approach left to the enemy were the north western and south eastern ends of the feature. An 'ad hoc' airdrop of ammunition, Bren guns and wireless batteries, was attempted just before dusk, using two light aircraft, but only a few items were recovered. A major airdrop was planned for 0900 the following morning, but in the event it could not take place because the Glosters were too heavily engaged when the aircraft arrived overhead. Fighter ground attack support was also promised at first light, as the battalion prepared for yet another night of action. Throughout the hours of darkness the enemy made a series of savage attacks, that were pressed home regardless of casualties, only be be beaten off by the defenders. However, the pressure was such that by dawn the Chinese were established in strength on the upper slopes of the hill, completely surrounding the Glosters' positions. The *Imjin Roll* continues:

Above: 'He inspired his officers and men to fight beyond the normal limits of human endurance, in spite of overwhelming odds and ever-increasing casualties, shortage of ammunition and water', so reads the citation to the award of the Victoria Cross to Lt-Col James Power Carne DSO, who commanded the 'Glorious Glosters'. He is seen here at Buckingham Palace, 27 October 1953. *IWM*

'The Chinese trumpets sounded all around . . . In retaliation the Adjutant suggested to the Colonel that the Drum Major might give them a reply. This he did and being the man he was, he was not going to do this crouched in a slit trench. Standing up ''Drummie'' Buss gave the Chinese the full repertoire. Long Reveille; Defaulters; Cookhouse; Officers Dress for Dinner; the Company calls — in fact everything except ''Retreat''. Buss was a good player and the notes of his bugle echoed over the Glosters position as dawn broke.*

---

* The bugle which 'Drummie' Buss used actually belonged to Anthony Eagles, who told me that it had been given to him by the Glosters depot before they left UK and it was the only one in the Regiment in Korea. After he had finished playing Buss returned the bugle and right at the end of the action, before he attempted to break out, Eagles used his last grenade to destroy it as he had no intention of allowing the bugle to be captured. '. . . I pulled the pin from my last grenade, framed it in the bell of the bugle and dropped it into my empty slit, where it exploded and blew the bugle to smithereens. I had no intention of allowing *that* bugle to be captured'.

As the light increased the Glosters could see their enemy. Hundreds of Chinese were milling around the slopes of their position. A Company in particular were hard pressed and were in danger of being pushed back. The Adjutant, Capt Farrar-Hockley, went forward to help, took control and organised a counter-attack. With magnificent support by the Gunners directed by Capt Ronnie Washbrook the position was retrieved. In a short period of an hour no less than seven attacks were repulsed.'

Among those stubborn defenders on top of Gloster Hill was L Cpl R. Haskell of Battalion HQ. He remembers his feelings thus:
'The order was given for Battalion HQ to leave its positions in the valley and to dig in on the hill. We carried as much ammo as we could and so began the last chapter of our three-day battle. The hill was covered with pine trees on one side and small bushes covering the other slopes. We had a good view of the valley below and were able to bring down fire on anything that moved there. I was in a slit trench with Cpl ''Taffy'' Watkins, our ACC cook, and soon

Above left: RSM Dee of the Glosters, who was a platoon sergeant in 1951 and was wounded on 25 April, pays his respects at the Gloster Hill War Memorial, April 1970. RSM Ivor Dee visited Korea together with RSM Norman Tuggey, who was also a platoon sergeant in the battle.
Brig A. D. R. G. Wilson

Above: RSM Ivor Dee, standing in front of the Korean hut in which he was held prisoner for about a month after the battle. Both he and RSM Tuggey were taken prisoner of the 26th, and eventually moved up to a PoW camp on the Yalu River in North Korea. They were not released until Operation 'Big Switch' in August 1953.
Brig A. D. R. G. Wilson

we and the rest of the lads were beating off repeated attacks with Mills bombs and Sten gun fire. All the time Chinese bugle calls could be heard around us, as if to let us know we were surrounded. As night fell a party led by RSM Hobbs made their way down to our transport and after a while managed to bring back food, water and ammo, which took some doing in the dark. At dawn on the second day we felt that we should give the Chinese a bugle lesson so the Drum Major sounded all the calls of the British Army and after that no more bugles were heard from the enemy. We were now running short of ammo and so an airdrop was asked for, but when the "Flying Boxcars" arrived overhead we could see that if they dropped anything 99% of it would fall into enemy hands, so the drop was called off. More and more attacks were launched against us, so airstrikes were called to help clear our forward slopes. We were told to cover ourselves with groundsheets as the US Air Force would be using Napalm bombs — that would warm somebody up, hopefully not us! The first aircraft made its run and let go the napalm right on target. It was followed by two more and then they came back to strafe the target with machinegun fire. It was a good job well done.'

By now the overall situation along the whole divisional front had badly deteriorated and a general withdrawal was ordered. A second attempt to relieve the Glosters never got off the ground and it became all too clear that the battalion was on its own and would have to find its own salvation. Accordingly, Col Carne gave orders that at 1030 hours the companies would attempt to break out independently and to reach the UN rearguard positions. All weapons and equipment that could not be carried would be destroyed, and, probably the hardest decision to make of all, that the wounded would have to be left behind. It almost goes without saying that Col Carne elected to stay behind with the wounded, as did the MO, Capt Bob Hickey, the Chaplain, Sam Davies, and the medical sergeant, Sgt 'Knocker' Brisland. 'Good luck and God Bless you all', said Cole Carne, as those unwounded began their escape attempts. L Cpl Haskell was one of the unlucky ones who did not evade capture:
'. . . so we were told to break out as best we could and to try to reach our own lines. A Task Force was trying to reach us, but they were held up some three miles away by strong Chinese forces. Down off the hill we came, snipers were having a field day and men began to drop on all sides. We made

our way along a rocky path until we could see that there really wasn't any chance of escape, so we were told to lay down our arms (after we had taken out the firing pins and broken the stocks with rocks). We were taken to the foot of the hill which is now called Gloster Hill and were very surprised to find the Chinese coming to meet us and shaking us by the hand and saying "Good Fight! Good Fight!" This was a sign of respect from one professional soldier to another — at least I like to think so. The battle was now all over and all was peaceful, but what lay ahead for us only time would tell.'

Anthony Eagles was one of the last to attempt to escape:
'. . . When I tried to break out, it was after the rest of the Regiment had gone. As a member of the Corps of Drums, we were the Defence Platoon and the last line of defence to headquarters. We stayed to look after the wounded until everyone had gone and there was nothing more we could do. We were out of ammunition and could not fight our way out, so it was "hide and seek". I was with the Intelligence Officer and the Drums Corporal. We took our rifles to pieces and buried the bits in different places . . . I was captured at the bottom of Gloster Hill.'

Pte Lionel Essex of B Company had the sort of adventures that sound as though they had come straight out of a novel, during the 27 days he spent behind the lines. Wounded by a piece of shrapnel in the head when he was trying to escape, he managed to get part of the way off the hill, but was wounded again this time in his left leg. While examining this wound he was hit a third time, in the right leg, and fell to the ground. He discovered that his right leg was broken, but continued down the hillside as best he could, crawling as he could no longer walk. Others tried to help him but, as he said afterwards, it was impossible for them to help much as it was all they could do to help themselves. He was joined at one time by his platoon sergeant, Sgt Robinson, who was also wounded in both the leg and arm. They stayed together until darkness fell and then Sgt Robinson went off down the hill to try to get help, but was captured, so Essex was again on his own. The next morning he was found by some Chinese who brutally interrogated him. When he refused to give anything but his number, rank, name and regiment, he was kicked and beaten and left lying on the hill. The following day they came again, and when he refused to tell them anything, kicked him repeatedly and finally threw a grenade at him - hitting him in the face, a penetrating wound above the eye, which broke the bone. The next day (26 April) he managed somehow to crawl the rest of the way down the hill and took refuge in a trench near the village of Paegun. Some villagers found him there and brought him food, however one of them was caught by the Chinese and shot. Despite this, one Korean boy of about 17 bravely continued to bring him food and water during the night, and Essex remained in the trench for about seven days. Eventually the Chinese found him lying there, but did not touch him. After they had gone he fortunately decided it was time to change hiding places and crawled painfully to another trench. Shortly after he had reached the new hiding place, the Chinese mortared his old one. Johnny, the Korean boy who had helped him each night, then took him into a house in the village and continued to care for him. Some days later there was an air strike and the family carried him out of the house and put him into another trench. The house was hit shortly afterwards by a napalm bomb and five Chinese who had been cooking inside were killed. Shortly afterwards the villagers managed to get Essex away and moved him to another village some 2½ miles to the north-west. Although Essex saw large numbers of Chinese in or near the village they appeared to take no interest in him, and it was clear that the villagers disliked the Chinese soldiers. On 20 May, a patrol from the Greek battalion that was probing forward to the Imjin, was told that a wounded British soldier was lying in a nearby village and being looked after by the villagers. Essex was found and taken back to hospital. When the Glosters reoccupied their old battalion positions at the end of May, they saw to it that the villagers were rewarded for all the help they had given to Essex. It appeared that the young Korean who had cared for him was probably one of the Battalion's porters.

An impressive list of awards for gallantry were made to the men of the Glosters and their attached personnel for this epic action, including two Victoria Crosses, two DSOs, one MBE, four MCs, two DCMs, 10 MMs and three BEMs, while the entire battalion and C Troop, 170th Independent Mortar Battery RA, was honoured by the United States with the award of a Presidential Unit Citation. Further awards were made to the men of the Glosters for gallant and distinguished service while they were prisoners, which included a George Cross, two MBEs and 10

Above: A 3 RAR mortar crew in action in the Pakchon battle. *Australian War Memorial*

BEMs. Of the 622-strong battalion that had first gone into action on 22 April 1951, only five officers and 41 other ranks remained, to begin with new replacements to rebuild the battalion. 'Only the Glosters could have done it,' is how their brigade commander described the stand of the Glosters which was in the very highest traditions of the British Army.

The Kapyong fight

While 29 Brigade was engaged in holding back the Chinese offensive on the Imjin River sector, 27 Brigade, some 30 miles to the east, was fighting its own desperate battle against overwhelming odds, with equal courage and fortitude. After taking part in the successful second advance northwards, the brigade had been relieved on 19 April by a regiment of the 6th ROK Division and pulled back to the area of Kapyong as part of IX Corps reserve. Their New Zealand gunners (NZ 16 Field Regiment) however, remained behind to support the South Koreans. During the night of 22/23 April, the Chinese and North Koreans launched heavy attacks and the ROK troops were soon forced to withdraw under pressure, in danger of being cut off and completely destroyed. NZ 16 Field Regiment had great difficulty in disengaging, but managed to do so and came into action again in the Kapyong valley, about four miles north of Chongon-ni. This was early on the 23rd, but a little later orders were given by IX Corps that the New Zealanders were to move forward again and support the South Koreans. The Brigade Commander (Brig B. A. Burke DSO) was given permission to send the 1st Middlesex with them for protection. Both

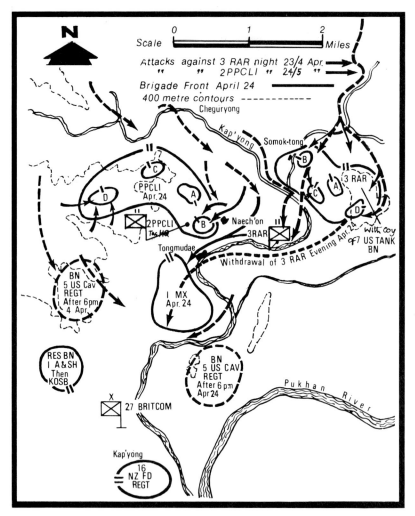

Above: The Kapyong fight, 23-25 April 1951.

Top right: Lt Leonard Montgomerie MC and men of his platoon (4 Platoon, B Company, 3 RAR) photographed after the Kapyong battle. Montgomerie and his men distinguished themselves in the battle, killing 81 Chinese in hand-to-hand fighting.
Australian War Memorial

Bottom right: A New Zealand Artillery Forward Observation Officer calls up support for the Australians.
Australian War Memorial

units moved about seven miles to the north-west and were quickly back in action. However, it soon became clear that the ROK 6th Division were continuing to retreat and that both units would soon be in a precarious position, so they were ordered back again. In the meantime, the rest of the brigade had been told to establish a defensive position astride the bend in the Kapyong River, just to the north of Chongchon-ni and the junction of the Kapyong and Pukhan Rivers.

The Kapyong valley is about 3,000 yards wide near the junction, but narrows as the river meanders to the north in wide sweeping curves. It is overlooked by Hill 677 to the west and Hill 504 to the east, and it was here that the brigadier established his forward battalions — 2nd Battalion, Princess Patricia's Canadian Light Infantry (PPCLI) left, on Hill 677, and 3rd Battalion, Royal Australian Regiment (RAR) on Hill 504, supported by A Company, US 72nd Heavy Tank Battalion. Brigade HQ was near Chongchon-ni, and just before midnight the Middlesex and the New Zealand gunners started withdrawing inside the brigade area. The other battalion of the

brigade, 1st Argyll and Sutherland Highlanders, had just been relieved by the 1st Battalion King's Own Scottish Borderers, who moved up on the 24th and took up reserve postions near Brigade HQ.

By 2200 on the 23rd the ROK resistance had completely crumbled and the leading Chinese troops were probing the brigade front, mostly in 3 RAR area. It was raining hard. By 0100 the Australians were under heavy attack from the north and north-west. Here is how the action that followed was described in the official Australian history of the Korean war entitled: *With the Australians in Korea*:

'The Australian front faced north-east, up the river valley and road. This was the direction from which the Chinese were expected to come — if they came. B Coy (Capt D. Laughlin), on the left of the road, had a loop of the river on its left flank, the road and paddy fields to the right. With B Coy on this island feature were a platoon of tanks from 72nd Heavy Tank Battalion, a machine gun section and fire observers from the US Independent 4.2in Chemical Mortar Battalion. Another platoon of tanks from the US tank battalion was forward from B Coy in flat country watching the road running in from the north-east. A Coy, under Maj B. S. O'Dowd, was in the centre position dug in along a high rocky spur. D Coy (Capt W. N. Gravener) was responsible for important high ground to the right of A Coy and C Coy (Capt R. W. Saunders) was in mobile reserve along a spur slightly west and to the rear of A Coy. Battalion HQ, with the pioneer platoon and the Bren gun section from the machine gun platoon, was about a mile SW of the company positions against some small hills 100 yards west of the road and south of Chuktun-ni village . . . Over on the isolated left flank B Coy had dug in comfortably enough. The battalion mail arrived just on dusk and the company cooks served a welcome hot meal. Capt Darcy Laughlin and his acting second in command, Lt J. H. Young, settled in Coy HQ, a large Australian Army pattern tent, and sampled a couple of bottles of beer. They could not rest because of the noise made by the retreating ROK's in the valley below. At 2000, Capt Laughlin sent a message by platoon runners to his platoon commanders which said: "There is nothing to worry about but step up security 50%." The chink and clink of picks and shovels sounded from the section positions as the forward platoons improved their defensive front.

'A Coy in the centre, had the most difficult ground and worked hard to prepare sangars and trenches before dark. The company's position was a long, low

ridge which rose sharply to a commanding bald knob in the east. No 1 Platoon (Lt F. A. Gardner) was nearest the road. Then came Coy HQ with the MMG section and, alongside them No 3 Platoon (Lt H. Mulry). No 2 Platoon (Lt I. R. W. Brumfield), occupied the bald knob overlooking the main position. By nightfall the platoons had cut defences into the unkind ground and the Quartermaster Sergeant (Sgt W. G. Mann) had organised a hot evening meal, after which F Echelon transport and the cooking gear returned to the rear. Sentries were posted and the remainder of the company curled up in sleeping bags before their turn came to watch. In the valley they could hear the disturbing sounds of retreating South Koreans. D Coy on the right had the highest ground. "Blue, our section leader, was always unlucky, so we got the biggest hill," wrote machine gunner Pte Eyre, "and we moved up with D Coy immediately. From the little flat we were in, right in the centre of the rice paddy, we climbed the highest of the hills, about two or three miles of backbreaking torture, carrying our Vickers guns, belts of ammo, our personal weapons, food and God alone

85

knows what else. At the crest we had a blow while Blue reported to Don Coy commander to find out exactly where we were to be situated. Meanwhile, we all parked around and nattered about everything except the thing that was uppermost in our minds: What's going to happen up here? How serious is the break-through? How long is this game going to last? Puffing and blowing Blue arrived back. 'On your feet fellers,' he said, 'we're going forward with No 11 Platoon to that high ridge there.' He motioned a ridge without a trace of vegetation on. 'Hell!' said Jack, one of the lads in the section, 'that hill reminds me of Harry's head, you can see it for miles.' Harry gave Jack a dirty look and we up the gear and off again until we were finally in position. We dug in and then Blue surveyed our pits and told us that a 50% stand-to was the order for the night. 'Keep your eyes open, he added, 'we don't know what to expect. He was right, we didn't know what to expect. But if a 50% stand-to was the order, we could expect something serious.''

'After dark the retreating South Koreans started to stream through the Australian positions, some at a jog-trot, others atop overloaded vehicles. Blaring horns and flashing lights added to the chaos, while intermittent gunfire could be heard from the Chinese who were advancing just behind the retreating Koreans. By 2200, the main Chinese force had reached the Australian perimeter. The US tank platoon in front of B Coy were the first to be engaged. Not quite clear as to whether it was the Chinese or the panic-stricken South Koreans who were shooting at them,

Above: Men of B Company, 3 RAR firing from slit trenches. *Australian War Memorial.*

Left: An M4A3 tank, belonging to the US 72nd Tank Battalion who supported 3 RAR so magnificently in the Kapyong battle, is seen here with ROK infantry during a demonstration of tank/infantry cooperation, 21 February 1952. *US Army*

the tanks fell back down the road between B Coy and the other company positions, towards the village of Chuktun-ni. Meanwhile the Chinese had fanned out and were probing all company positions, and with the tanks out of position, pushing down the road towards Bn HQ. The US tank commander, who had given no orders to his forward platoon to withdraw, rushed into the valley to stop them pulling back too far. Lt Young (2IC B Coy) went with him: "We reached the road too late to stop two of the tanks from falling back to Bn HQ area," wrote Lt Young, describing what happened next. "We stopped the last one. The commander said that he had dead and wounded aboard and was going back to recrew and rearm. We persuaded him to stop and promised to send his wounded back by jeep and bring ammunition up to him. The tank skipper then asked where we wanted him to stop and block. A rather indefinitive wave of the arm on my part was not sufficient for him. He wanted to be guided to his position. That left me posted so I marched ahead of the tank *north* along the road. By this time an American mortar FFO (Forward Fire Officer) accompanied by a negro carrying his wireless set, had joined us. The FFO was looking for our A Coy and wanted guiding. After walking for about 50 yards, with the tank grinding along behind us in the dark, I saw movement in the shadow of a bank on the right side of the road, toward A Coy. There was moonlight on the road itself. Thinking that ROK troops were still skulking there I called up 'Iddiwa' (Anglicised Korean for 'Come Here'). A train of sparks flying towards me through the air was the

answer. I dived for the ditch on the left of the road. The FFO and his wireless man went for the hill towards A Coy. The tank driver immediately put his vehicle into reverse gear and went backwards. The grenade burst harmlessly on the road. I was now reasonably sure that the Chinese were with us and against us. As I lay in the ditch the Chinese Communist Forces literally ran over me after the tank down the road. They flung a few grenades in my direction but did no harm beyond singeing my moustache and hair. I lay quiet for some time, whilst the noise of pursuit faded south, then I cautiously made my way back to B Company lines."

'Meanwhile fighting had flared up right around the battalion perimeter and inside the headquarters area. The main Chinese drive swept down the valley to the ford and established a road block behind HQ. The initial attack killed two Bren gunners and wounded four others, besides causing casualties among the regimental police, and signallers who were defending the low ground around the ford. Lt C. B. Evans, commanding the MG Platoon, saved the situation by asking an American tank commander to turn his cannon on the road block and nearby houses. This tank fire killed 40 Chinese in one house alone. Strong Chinese pressure continued throughout the night and all companies suffered heavy casualties. The enemy who had been thwarted at the ford fell back to renew their attacks against the forward rifle companies. At about 0430 hours, a company of the Middlesex supported by tanks, tried to get up to reinforce the pioneer platoon position, which was the

Below: 2nd PPCLI move forward for a second attack on Point 419, 24 February 1951. The battalion were awarded a Presidential Unit Citation for their gallantry in the Kapyong battle, April 1951.
Public Archives Canada

key to the Battalion HQ position, but were unable to do so, due to heavy enemy pressure. Fortunately as daylight came the situation eased. Enemy attacks continued throughout the 24th, they lost heavily but still came on. Helping the MO was Salvation Army Major Edwin Robertston, but when he saw there were not enough stretcher bearers to bring in the mounting casualties, he went out with the hygiene corporal ("Gunner" McMurray MM) to bring in the more seriously wounded. Often they had to crawl on their hands and knees with the stretcher as they visited the front line. "As always seems to be the case during the fiercest battle, humour crept in", wrote Maj Robertson later, "some of the forward troops noticed a lone Chinaman making his way over a ridge to obtain a commanding position from which he could snipe our lines. A sergeant, attached to the support company saw him and fired, but only kicked up the dust at the Chinaman's feet. This sergeant was always known as a good shot so some of the boys chaffed him. Full of determination, he had

another shot and the same thing happened. Again the boys barracked him and this time, with a do or die glint in his eye, he fired again but only to see the same again. Then, to his amazement, the Chinaman whipped off his shirt, tied it to his rifle, and waved a 'Washout' which highly amused the Australians and helped to relieve the tension."'

The enemy, now identified as the 188th Division CCF, continued their heavy attacks, and, when it became evident that 3 RAR would be unable to sustain another night attack, they were ordered to withdraw. This movement began about 1730 and was closely followed by the enemy. However, pressure was considerably lessened by the accurate artillery and tank fire. By about 2245, the Australians had passed through the Middlesex and taken up new positions near Brigade HQ. For good measure they brought 32 Chinese prisoners with them! Here is how the official history describes the fighting withdrawal:

Below: Guns of the 2nd Regiment RCHA fire in support of a patrol from 2nd Royal Canadian Regiment towards Hill 730, 21 June 1951. In foreground an M2A1 half track.
Public Archives Canada

'. . . Taking advantage of this unexpected support* the Chinese launched a frontal attack coupled with a flanking movement to the right. No 11 platoon held off the frontal attack and made a minor adjustment to counter the attempted right flank move. Once again the enemy suffered heavy casualties and drew back. At this stage, D Coy was acting as a rearguard covering the withdrawal of the other companies along high ground to the reserve area occupied by Bn HQ and the Middlesex. D Coy received its orders to withdraw late in the afternoon but was then beating off one of the heaviest attacks of the day. "This was the most determined attack we had experienced up to then," Capt Graverner wrote in a report of the action. "The enemy fairly ran headlong into our forward lines and, on the right, had gained the cover of a spur but could not breach our position. At this critical stage it was decided to begin thinning out. We completed this action according to the book and although always followed up we suffered no further casualties except one man reported missing. During this thinning out process, the New Zealand artillery slowed down the enemy follow-up. Corrections to bring this artillery fire as close as possible were very effective. As we finally cleared feature 504, which was at the south end of the main ridge, shells were falling no more than 150 yards forward of our troops. At this stage, Maj Hunt took over artillery fire direction and the volume of fire completely frustrated enemy attempts to follow-up further so that the withdrawal was speeded up without further incident." Throughout the night of 23 April and all next day, D Coy had no direct communications with Battalion HQ. Capt Gravener kept contact through Maj O'Dowd and A Coy signals. After the napalm attack of the afternoon of 24 April even requests for tank support had to go through A Coy. This meant that Maj O'Dowd directed the withdrawal, in which D Coy acted as rearguard. By just after 2100 on the night of 24 April, the rifle companies were all clear of the forward feature which they had defended so successfully for a night and a day.

'During the night of 23 April and all day on 24 April, American tanks, commanded by Lt Kenneth W. Koch, collaborated closely with the Australian troops. One tank platoon commander, Lt Wilfred D. Miller, won the Distinguished Service Cross for his courage and initiative during the first Chinese attack. This assault, early on the night of 23 April, killed the forward tank platoon commander and wounded three tank commanders. When the platoon began to fall back in some disorder, Lt Miller, advancing with his own platoon, jumped from the protection of his own tank and ran forward to halt the retreat and direct the tanks to alternative positions. On the following day Lt Miller repeatedly led his platoon through enemy-held territory to carry critically needed ammunition and supplies to the Australian companies and to evacuate wounded. "My platoon nearest D Coy came into the fray as the enemy attacked D Coy", wrote Capt Saunders, when paying tribute to the American tanks. "D Coy stood firm and my fellows said it was better than the fun parlour at Luna Park. However, one great problem soon presented itself. The ammunition was running low and we were beginning to have casualties. About this time, away to the south, I could see dust coming from behind a hill that concealed the road. Then our American tank friends reappeared around the corner, bringing us fresh ammunition and lots of morale. They evacuated our wounded and made several trips along this two-mile stretch of road, under fire the whole way. They never once faltered and they helped to build up a strong bond of respect between the fighting men of the two countries. Towards evening orders came to withdraw. We did so, ably supported by our Anzac friends of the New Zealand 16th Field Artillery. As D Coy evacuated their positions Chinese troops were right behind them and many a Chinaman had a dead heat or photo finish with a 25pdr Kiwi shell. Sometimes the Chinaman won and sometimes only came second. On the road to the west were the faithful tanks watching us withdraw as darkness fell, leaving them alone, surrounded by Chinese infantry, and infantry are deadly against tanks at night. Several hours later, we came to the Middlesex lines, passed through them and on Anzac Eve we dug in among friends. At last I felt like an Anzac and I imagine there were 600 others like me." This ended the battle for the Australians. They had held their positions all night and all day, exhausting and demoralising the Chinese and gradually blunting their offensive. The Australian casualties had been heavy — 31 killed, 58 wounded and three missing later known to have been taken prisoner, but they had played their part magnificently.'

*The 'support' was in fact a napalm attack by a flight of Corsairs which had unfortunately landed on D Coy, causing casualties and destroying vital weapons and ammunition. Capt M. Ryan ran out under fire waving the indentification panel which had been on the ground to mark the position, while the coy radio operator made frantic efforts to save his radio set — the only link to the artillery fire support.

Until the withdrawal of the Australians, the 2nd PPCLI had remained relatively undisturbed. The battalion had deployed to cover the north face of Hill 677, with A Coy right, C Coy centre and D Coy left. B Coy occupied a salient in front of D Coy. At 0400 24 April, the CO, Lt-Col J. R. Stone DSO, MC, set up his tactical headquarters on the rear slope of the hillside, overlooking the thatched village of Tungmudae, the companies had already been in position some six hours. At 0700 a small body of enemy were reported just in rear of Battalion HQ and to meet this threat Col Stone moved B Coy further south, to a hill immediately east of Tac HQ. The American tanks, which were engaged in supporting the Australian regiment's withdrawal, unfortunately opened fire in error on B Coy as it occupied the hill, slightly wounding one man. From its new position B Coy was able to observe the movement of the enemy across the wide Kapyong valley to the north and east and in the area of the village of Neach'on. This movement increased during the day and at about 2200 enemy mortar bombs began to fall on the PPCLI position, two machine guns opened up at long range and a third MG began to range on to B Coy with tracer, evidently as a direction marker. Within a quarter of an hour the forward platoon of B Coy (No 6) was under heavy attack by at least 200 enemy. Here is how the battle is described in the official Canadian history of the war, entitled *Strange Battleground* reproduced by kind permission of the Minister of Supply and Services, Canada:

'The battalion mortars and the company machine guns stopped this assault within a few yards of the company perimeter. At 2300 the attack was renewed, preceded as before by a few mortar bombs. This time the forward platoon of B Coy was partially overrun, but most of the men were able to fight their way back to the main company position, where they were organised into a counter-attack force which succeeded in stopping the enemy thrust. As the attack was in progress against B Coy, about 100 Chinese probed at the Tac HQ and the battalion mortars from a gully in the rear of the position. Maj Lilley (OC B Coy) had recorded his impression of this attack: "The probe against Battalion HQ was a well-executed attack in strength which I estimated at that time to be between one and two companies and which B Coy was powerless to stop as it came in through the back door. It was a heartening sight to see the battalion mortars firing at their shortest range (200yd) together with their .50 calibre machine guns which literally blew the Chinese back down the ravine."

'Shortly afterwards a larger body of enemy was caught in a heavy concentration of artillery fire as it forded the Kapyong. The Patricias on the hill saw them clearly in the moonlight as the broke and fled. The Canadians counted 71 Chinese dead on the river banks next morning. During these attacks on B Coy, Pte W. R. Mitchell, a Bren gunner, distinguished himself by the skill and resolution which he displayed in performing his fire tasks. From the moment the first attacks came in, Mitchell was at work with his Bren and was largely responsible for repulsing the enemy attacking No 6 Platoon. He was wounded in the chest early in the battle but after having the wound dressed he continued to fight, firing from the hip and moving from fire trench to fire trench as the enemy pressed towards platoon HQ, until he was again wounded. The second wound did nothing to deter him and he continued to fight for the rest of the night. In the words of the recommendation: "At daylight Pte Mitchell could hardly stand for loss of blood." He was evacuated by helicopter and subsequently awarded the Distinguished Conduct Medal. By 0200 every weapon in the battalion was firing on the Chinese and it became apparent that the attack on B Coy and Bn HQ — savage though it had been — was only diversionary. D Coy, in its exposed position on the north-west, was attacked by large numbers of the enemy from two sides and the waves of Chinese succeeded in infiltrating the area in strength. This action is best described by quoting from the report of Capt J. G. W. Mills, the company commander: "Shortly after last light we heard an amazingly large volume of small arms fire from the direction of Tac HQ and B positions. This fire finally subsided until we could hear only the occasional burst. At approximately 0110 hours we received word via the wireless, from Lt Levy, 10 Platoon commander, that Cpl Clouthier had reported the enemy were assembled in the saddle known as 'FOX THREE' (an artillery fire task codeword). Immediately we received this word, we heard a Bren from 10 Platoon open fire. I called for fire task FOX THREE. Levy asked the MMG in the 12 Platoon position to open fire on the enemy. The machine gunners immediately fired on the enemy with such deadly accuracy that the enemy stopped his main attack on 10 Platoon. The enemy then directed his main assault against the MMG thus relieving the pressure on 10 Platoon. In their attack on 10 Platoon the enemy used machine guns and mortars to cover their assault. The enemy then attacked across the small saddle overrunning one section of 12 Platoon and the MMG. This was accomplished by sheer weight of numbers. The machine guns continued to fire until the crew was completely overrun. Four men from the 12 Platoon section which was protecting the MMG post were able to disengage and make their way over to 10 Platoon positions where they carried on the firefight. They reported that the two machine gunners had been killed at their posts. Also two Koreans, who comprised part of the MMG section, were able to make their way to 10 Platoon positions. The enemy having gained possession of our MMG endeavoured to use it, but 10 Platoon covered the gun and the position with LMG fire by Pte Baxter and rendered the MMG useless. Sgt Holigan reported that the enemy were building up in the area known as fire task ABLE ONE. We asked for fire on FOX THREE and ABLE ONE, as this seemed the main line of approach.''

'At this critical moment Capt Mills requested the artillery to lay down defensive fire on top of his position and after two hours succeeded in stemming the enemy's advance. Undeterred by these reverses, the enemy persisted in his attacks, but was driven off each time by artillery fire. At last, with the approach of daylight, the pressure subsided and D Coy was able to re-establish itself in its previous position. Capt Mills was awarded the Military Cross for his bravery in this action. Pte K. F. Barwise of C Coy was awarded the Miliary Medal for the courage he displayed during the reoccupation of the position, in particular for his single-handed recapture of the MMG. By contrast with the night, the daylight hours of 25 April were quiet. The 2nd PPCLI held its lonely hill and although it was subjected to heavy fire, remained free from attack. The battalion was, however, cut off from the rest of the brigade — the supply route to the rear was held by the enemy — and the ammunition and emergency rations had been depleted. Failing normal supply, Stone requested an air drop.

'The message had to go up the chain of command and across to a base in Japan, but at 10.30, only six hours after the request had been made, four C-119 aircraft dropped the right proportions of British

Below: Vehicles of US 2nd Infantry Division destroyed during the Chinese Spring Offensive. *US Army*

and American ammunition and a supply of rations. Only four parachutes dropped outside the battalion area. At 1400 patrols from B Coy reported the road clear, and Stone requested that additional supplies be brought up by vehicle as soon as possible. By late afternoon on the 25th the area was quiet and the battalion was able to take stock of the situation. It had maintained its positions intact, and these positions covered the ground vital to the defence of the brigade area. In addition, its relatively light casualties of 10 killed and 23 wounded testified to the skill with which the position had been organised and defended. Lt-Col Stone's outstanding leadership during this action led to the award of a second bar to his Distinguished Service Order.'

Reviewing the battle, the Intelligence Staff at UN Command estimated that at least two Chinese regiments (about 6,000 men) had attacked 27 Brigade and had suffered terrible casualties in their abortive attacks. Undoubtedly the stand at Kapyong stopped the Chinese advance in this sector and forced them to look elsewhere for tactical gains. 'The seriousness of the break-

through on the central front had been changed from defeat to victory by the gallant stand of these heroic and courageous soldiers,' so reads the Presidential Unit Citation, '... The 3rd Battalion, Royal Australian Regiment, the 2nd Battalion, Princess Patricia's Canadian Light Infantry and A Company, 72nd US Heavy Tank Company, displayed such gallantry, determination and *esprit de corps* in accomplishing their missions as to set them apart and above other units participating in the campaign, and by their achievements they have brought distinguished credit to themselves, their homelands and all freedom-loving nations.'

Formation of 1st Commonwealth Division

The next three months saw a period of comparative quiet for the British and Commonwealth soldiers. This allowed both the 28th* and 19th Brigades to reorganise and settle down after their battles. It also allowed the 25th Canadian Brigade to be assembled under reasonably settled conditions, and for all three brigades to be suitably grouped and located for the formation of the Commonwealth Division. The staff of Divisional HQ had begun to arrive from all over the globe in early June. Maj-Gen A. J. H. Cassels CB, CBE, DSO, Division Commander designate, reached Japan on 11 June (he had paid a flying visit to Korea two months before that). The main body of Divisional HQ reached Pusan towards the end of July and moved up country. At midday on 28 July 1951, a short ceremony was held near Tokchong, which was attended by the Commander of the Eighth Army, Gen James A. Van Fleet, and the C-in-C British Commonwealth Forces in Japan, Lt-Gen Sir Horace Robertson, to mark the formation of the Division. Here, for the first time a Commonwealth Divison flag was raised. As Brig C. N. Barclay explains in his history of the Division, *The First Commonwealth Division:* 'In the course of the next two years many changes were made among units and personnel: but the Division's truly Commonwealth character was not altered, and the Commonwealth spirit was maintained throughout. Men from many countries and of many races and creeds, were to support each other in battle, deliver each other's rations, ammunition and stores and tend each other's wounded — all part of the armed forces of the great association of nations which had been built up over the centuries with so much toil and good will.'

Right: Maj-Gen A. J. H. Cassels, popularly known by his soldiers as 'Gentleman Jim', first commander of the Commonwealth Division.
US Army

* At midnight of 25/26 April 1951 the 27th Commonwealth Infantry Brigade had changed its designation to the 28th Commonwealth Brigade (its composition remaining unchanged).

Stabilising the front

Although such actions as those of 27 and 29 Brigades had halted the Chinese pressure, this was not to be their last attack. In fact it was discovered from the interrogation of prisoners, that it was but the first of a three stage assault planned by the enemy with the aim of driving the UN forces right out of Korea. The next major offensive was launched in mid-May, when no less than 26 enemy divisions (23 CCF and three North Korean) launched strong attacks all along the front. For three days the enemy, having driven back the UN covering forces, fought savagely to break through the main defensive line in the central sector. This was followed by heavy attacks in the eastern sector, and although the Chinese made some progress, they suffered terrible casualties. By the end of May it was estimated that the enemy had lost over 100,000 men killed and wounded, 12,000 captured together with large quantities of stores and equipment. 16 of their divisions were down to 50% fighting strength and they had been so badly shattered as to make them incapable of further offensive operations. Small wonder therefore, that the Eighth Army was able to take over the offensive once more and to press the enemy northwards again. By

Below: Cpl Leonard Wolper, medic, gives aid to Pvt Roger M. Silvernails, while under heavy fire on Hill 364, near T'Omok-Kol, 24 May 1951. Both were in the 31st Infantry Regiment, 7th US Infantry Division. *US Army*

mid-June, the UN forces were again back across the 38th Parallel and had just about stabilised the front.

It is hardly surprising that the Communists considered this an opportune moment to bring up the question of peace talks. Action at the front did not of course end, even though both sides were busy establishing their defensive lines. To illustrate this are two stories, the first being an example of how, in Korea, even non-combatant units often found themselves having to fight for their lives. This is followed by an account of US Infantry units attacking 'Heartbreak Ridge' — one of the many hundreds of Korean hills which received its own special codename.

Fighting medics

Sometimes even the normally non-combatant medical corpsmen had to be prepared to fight for their lives in Korea. One such occasion concerned the medical company of the 21st Infantry Regiment, 24th Infantry Division, in May 1951. The Eighth Army counter-offensive that month had driven the Communist divisions back across the 38th Parallel, inflicting many casualties and capturing much booty. It was, however, known that a good many enemy groups and stragglers had been bypassed by the attack, so administrative units had to take precautions against attack. The company had a permanent guard force of 20 men and when the medics set up their tents, they put out four two man posts, as per SOPs (Standard Operating Procedures). The medics were about 300 yards from the regimental

command post and about the same distance from the gun positions of A Battery, 213th Armoured Field Artillery Battalion. The campsite was on the side of a hill in a narrow strip between the place where the steep slope ended and, continuing below it, the terraced rice paddies began. A little to the south-east of the company position, a small stream came down through a defile in the hill mass. Early on the morning of 27 May, some enemy stragglers moved down along the small stream and through the defile, clearly trying to find their way back to their own lines. Here is how the resulting action is described in *Combat Support in Korea*:

'At about 0200, the foremost of the enemy soldiers ran into the medical company's guards along the stream bank. One guard challenged the first Chinese soldier he heard or saw, and got a volley of concussion grenades for his trouble. The explosions awakened the rest of the company. Some were sleeping in tents, some on cots and stretchers, and some in trucks. The first reaction of everyone above ground was to get down. The second was to get dressed before going out in the mud and rain to meet the enemy.

'The five officers and 63 medics were inadequately armed for combat. In fact, only a few had ammunition. Sgt Vincenzo DiSanto had a little on the supply truck and put out the first 150 rounds to three guards who came asking for some. This left him with 250 rounds of carbine ammo and eight grenades. DiSanto decided to leave his truck and pass out the ammunition to those who needed it. He found that a firing line had already been built up. The ground was such that the only cover was behind a retaining wall a few yards west of the company. This put the company's tents and vehicles right between the firing line and the enemy. In a few minutes DiSanto distributed his small supply of ammunition. He kept one grenade for himself to supplement his pistol. The enemy was not organised. One group moved down the stream bed and set up a roadblock. Others fanned out and ran into Battery A and the medical company. In the confusion our troops were fearful of hitting one another. As Lt John Atkins visited a post near the stream he heard the guard challenge, yelling, "Who are you?" "ROK soldiers," the reply came, so Atkins shouted to the guard, "Hold your fire!" He quickly changed his mind when the "ROK soldiers" opened up with burp guns. Several enemy soldiers got into the company area and threw grenades. The grenades were ineffective and led only to the throwers being killed. The cooks in

their white clothing, seemed to attract the attention of the enemy more than anyone else. In the shooting, enough rounds were fired by both sides to riddle all the company tents. The firing line of the medical company was never seriously threatened. The chief effect of its fire seemed to have been to deflect the enemy on the medical company's side of the stream into the line of the regimental CP on the left of the company area. A runner sent over to regiment to report the fight found the CP was fighting too.

'Sporadic fire continued until daylight. The company reorganised at dawn. A nose count showed 58 Chinese prisoners and 23 enemy dead in and around the company position. Casualties of the company were one killed and 10 wounded, and the regimental chaplain (Father Francis X.

Top: Men of C Squadron 7 RTR brew up, while their Churchill tank stands in the background. Although the Churchills were equipped with flamethrowers and trailers, they were only used as gun tanks. In many respects the Churchills proved ideal because of their excellent cross-country performance in bad conditions. *IWM*

Above: 8th Hussar Centurions carry men of the Royal Northumberland Fusiliers on a fighting patrol. *IWM*

Coppens) was killed in the company area. Companies F and G, 5th Infantry came on the scene shortly after daybreak and, accompanied by two self-propelled guns, counterattacked. Several men of the medical force joined this force. A hundred prisoners were soon taken, and the POW bag for the 5th Infantry and 21st Infantry during the day was 2,900. The medical company continued to work during the firefight. Lt Edward Green USNR (the acting regimental surgeon)* was wounded on the firing line. He went to the first-aid tent with the other wounded. There he treated these men and remained to treat others as they were brought in. An officer-patient, awaiting evacuation, was rewounded as he lay on a stretcher. The Chinese were more surprised than the men of the medical company. Intent only on escaping encirclement, they were unable to launch an organised assault. Had they been able to do so, they would certainly have overrun the lightly armed troops. Nevertheless, the determination of the medical company to resist the assault helped prevent the enemy escaping. By 0830 the company was extremely cocky. They were "fighting medics" and wanted to know: "Who the hell says the medics can't fight?"'

Heartbreak Ridge

The codename 'Heartbreak Ridge' had been given to a seven-mile long hill mass

* During this period the US Army borrowed 500 Naval Reserve physicians, some of whom saw active service in Korea. Whenever a Navy officer was the senior officer in a unit, he commanded it.

which was an important part of the enemy defensive positions in October 1951. One of the subsidiary positions protecting this ridgeline was Hill 520, a hump at the western end of the spur that jutted out from the main ridgeline. Fighting for this feature came at the end of a month-long battle for Heartbreak Ridge.

By 10 October 1951, UN forces had secured the steep part of the spur ridge that slanted down towards Hill 520. Still in enemy hands, however, was the end of the ridge, a series of bumps ending in the highest, which was Hill 520, at the very end of the blunt tip of the ridge. The task of seizing this hump was given by Eighth Army to X Corps, who passed it down to the 2nd Infantry Division, thence to the 23rd Infantry Regiment, who selected G Company to make the attack. The fighting on Heartbreak Ridge had been so severe that at one time G Company numbered 23 men. However, by 10 October, enough reinforcements had joined to bring each of its platoons up to a strength of about 20 men each. The company commander was in Japan for five days 'R&R' (Rest and Rehabilitation, ie leave, but known by most people as 'Rack & Ruin' — a tribute to the fleshpots of Japan!) so Lt Raymond W. Riddle, the combat experienced executive officer, was in command for the attack. He decided to make his first move with 3 Platoon (Cpl David Lamb was acting platoon leader). Here is how the attack is described in *Combat Actions in Korea*:

'The other two rifle companies from the 2nd Battalion were in positions to support the attack. Company F, located on the same ridge just behind Lt Riddle's men,

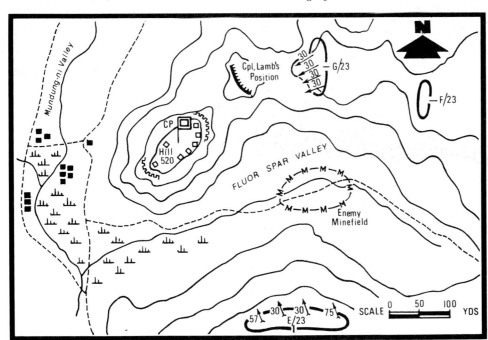

Far left: Vigil on a Korean ridgetop. A Forward Air Control Unit with the 1st US Marine Division scans the sky anxiously for incoming close air support. *US Marine Corps*

Left: Heartbreak Ridge, 10 October 1951.

was prepared to pass through Company G and continue the attack if necessary. Company E was to support the attack by firing from a parallel ridge 500 yards to the south. The flat top of Hill 520 was not more than 200 yards beyond Company G's line of departure. On the ridgeline, about halfway between these two points was a small knoll. After considering an envelopment of the enemy position by sending Cpl Lamb's platoon into the Fluor Spar Valley — a narrow strip of flat land between his position and Company E on the next ridge south, and so named because of the fluorspar (the mineral fluorite) mines in the valley — Riddle decided to make a direct assault along the ridgeline. There were enemy minefields in the valley. He could see some enemy movement on the objective. Hoping to draw fire so that he could estimate the enemy strength there, Lt Riddle ordered everyone in the company — including the mortarmen — to fire on the objective for 30 seconds. The enemy did not, however, return the fire.

'When this ruse failed, Lt Riddle called for supporting fire from the artillery, heavy machine guns and Company F's 57mm recoilless rifles. At about 1300, after 10 or 15 minutes of preparation, he stopped the artillery and instructed Cpl Lamb to double-time his platoon to the intermediate knoll under cover of fire from the machine guns, the recoilless rifles and the other riflemen in Company G. Once there, he was to set up a platoon base of fire and make

Above: 25pdr towed by a Quad tractor. *IWM*

Left: The mortar squad of 2nd Platoon, Recce Company, 3rd Infantry Division gets into position on Hill 130, while men of G and H Companies 65th Infantry Regiment, move forward to stem the fifth Chinese offensive, 23 April 1951. *US Army*

Above right: Sgt First Class Jack B. Moore uses his sniper rifle, north of Inje, 29 May 1951. Note the flash hider and telescopic sight. *US Army*

Right: A group of riflemen, armed with the .30 M1 rifle, belonging to 65th RCT, 3rd US Infantry Division, are but a small part of the massive firepower along the new UN defence line, north of the 38th Parallel, 1 June 1951. *US Army*

the final assault on the objective. Moving out quickly, Lamb's platoon reached the knob without difficulty. The machine gun crew set up its weapon and opened fire on the main objective. After deploying his platoon around the base of the knoll, Lamb reported back to Lt Riddle: "No casualties yet, but receiving plenty of fire." In response to Lamb's request, Riddle instructed the support elements to intensify their fire, especially on the south side of the objective. PFC Harry E. Schmidt, who was in Cpl Lamb's platoon, had a yellow panel wrapped around his waist. His mission was to stay with the lead assault elements so that the supporting elements would know where the platoon was. Although conspicuous himself, Schmidt made it easy for the rest of his company and for men of Company E to identify the most forward position of the attacking platoon. While the rest of the platoon fired at bunkers on the east end of the hill, Cpl Lamb sent one squad around the left side of the objective. Brisk enemy fire drove the squad back to the platoon base, proving that both the preparatory and supporting fires had been ineffective against the enemy bunkers. Several men from the attacking squad were wounded, and enemy fire, reaching back to the intermediate knob, had caused several other casualties there. Cpl Lamb radioed to Lt Riddle for reinforcements. Loading the 1st Platoon with ammunition, Riddle committed it to assist in the attack. Lt Jay M. Gano, a recent replacement, commanded 1st Platoon. Since he was inexperienced in combat, he had instructed Pvt Cliff R. High, who had been running the platoon, to continue to do so for the time being.

'As the 1st Platoon crawled towards Lamb's position, two men were wounded not far beyond the line of departure. One of them, seriously wounded in the face and neck by a machine gun bullet, became hysterical, and it was necessary for High to hold him down. Farther forward, Lt Gano, with the lead elements of his platoon, had almost reached the intermediate knoll when he was killed on this his first attack. The platoon halted, pinned down by hostile fire. Just at this time Cpl Lamb's machine gun ceased firing. ''I'm out of ammo!'' the gunner shouted. Seven or eight enemy soldiers came out of their bunkers and suddenly appeared on the slope of Hill 520 descending toward Lamb's platoon. He reported that he was being counter-attacked. Supporting machine gun fire was too high to be effective. Lamb's riflemen opened fire, the ammunition bearers fired their carbines, and even the machine gunner fired his pistol. Part way down the slope the enemy soldiers stopped, and turned back. A brush fire had started in the area between Lamb and the company's original position. The haze and smoke drifted north over High's immobilised platoon, making it impossible for Lt Riddle to see the objective. Taking a chance, Riddle ordered his machine guns at the line of departure to fire on Hill 520. Lamb reported back that the machine gun fire was 'Just right!' Under cover of the machine gun fire and the smoke from the brush fire, High, having calmed the wounded man, sent him and another casualty to the rear and then worked his platoon forward, meeting eight or ten wounded men from Lamb's platoon who were working their way back to the company. Cpl Lamb needed more machine gun ammunition and Lt Riddle sent a squad from the 2nd Platoon with eight boxes. In the meantime, Lamb and High planned their assault.

'Seven enemy mortar shells now fell among High's platoon, wounding six more men. High sent them to the rear. He now had 11 men besides himself, Lamb had

about 12. After the ammunition arrived, the two platoon leaders, leaving six men to man the machine gun and fire rifles from the intermediate knoll, called off their long range supporting fire and then assaulted with the remaining men deployed in a skirmish line, firing as they moved forward. 60 yards of open ground lay between the jump-off point and the enemy trenches on the slope of the objective. All went well until halfway across the enemy commenced firing automatic weapons. This fire was not effective, however, and did not stop the advance. When the skirmish line reached base of the knoll, enemy soldiers stopped firing and began throwing fragmentation and concussion grenades. These caused trouble. One of the grenades wounded Lamb. Cpl Arne Severson, seeing the skirmish line falter, picked up his machine gun and walked forward, firing as he advanced. When he reached the base of the hill an enemy grenade exploded at this feet and broke both his legs. But he set up his gun and continued to fire until the attack stalled. Two men dragged him back. High moved the remaining members of both platoons back to a covered position

and radioed Lt Riddle to bring in the machine gun fire again and to send help, if possible. North Korean soldiers in the bunkers on the objective began to taunt High and his men with phrases such as ''American you die!''. Deciding to make a second attempt — this time a close-in envelopment of the objective — High called off the supporting fire again and led about a dozen of his men downhill toward the south, where they could move without being seen or fired upon by the enemy. They then climbed the hill, moving north to the top of Hill 520. When the men broke defilade, the enemy opened fire and began throwing grenades again. A concussion grenade knocked High down. The rest of his men, believing him dead, straggled back to the platoon base. Within a minute or two, however, High regained conciousness and returned to the platoon base where he reorganised the remaining men — about 20 in all.

'In the meantime, regimental HQ had sent three flamethrower operators to the 2nd Battalion two of them designated for Company G and one for Company F. Lt Riddle sent all three men, with their

Top left: Company C, 7th RCT, 3rd Infantry Division, enter a village near Uijong-bu, 5 May 1951. *US Army*

Centre left: A .50cal heavy machine gun of Company H, 9th Infantry Regiment, 2nd Infantry Division, gives covering fire to a returning patrol near Chunchon, 7 May 1951. *US Army*

Bottom left: Men of 1st Battalion, 7th RCT, 3rd Infantry Division on the side of Hill 117 shortly after they had captured it. The Chinese still hold the surrounding hills, 3 July 1951. *US Army*

Below: Men of B and C Companies, 23rd Infantry Regiment, US 2nd Infantry Division, work on a communications trench along the slope of Old Baldy ridge. *US Army*

flamethrowers strapped to their backs, forward to help High. One operator was wounded almost immediately upon leaving the line of departure; the other two reached High as he was preparing to make another assault. He sent one flamethrower operator and two riflemen directly to the front. Under cover of fire, the men crawled into positions from where they could place flame on the foremost bunker (the eastern one) on Hill 520. As soon as this bunker was destroyed, High led the rest of his platoon around to the left and formed a skirmish line facing another enemy bunker on the south side of the hill. In position, he signalled the flamethrower to open up. As soon as the flamethrower commenced operating, High was to signal the assault. This time the flamethrower failed to work. By then only two enemy bunkers were interfering with the attack. A machine gun was firing from each. High decided to make the assault without the flamethrower. He sent a BAR team to knock out the bunker while he, with the rifleman and the third flamethrower operator, walked toward the other. Firing as they walked, the men exposed themselves because High feared that if they tried to crawl they would be pinned down. Ten yards from the bunker, the second flamethrower failed to work. Standing exposed to enemy fire, the operator took it apart but was unable to repair it. Finally High told him to get out of the way because he was too conspicuous. High stationed one of his riflemen in front of the bunker. Unable to hit anyone in it, he nevertheless prevented the North Koreans from firing and thus neutralised the pos-

ition. Just about that time an automatic weapon began firing from another bunker on the left, and High told Pvt Joe Golinda to get it. Golinda approached it from one side, High from another, while a third man covered them. Golinda threw a grenade into the bunker, and the gun stopped firing. With only a few men firing rifles and BARs for support, High and four or five men made the final assault on the top of Hill 520. Pvt Schmidt, still wearing the yellow panel wrapped around his waist, stayed up with the foremost men as he had throughout the attack. The group moved on around the hill, firing into the apertures of three other bunkers. All were empty. Once they reached the top of the hill the men saw eight enemy soldiers running over the hill toward the north-west, and opened fire on them. On the north side of the hill High came upon a bunker that had been the enemy's command post. Eight enemy soldiers, still holding their weapons, were huddled in the bunker. When High's men fired into the group the North Koreans threw up their hands and surrendered themselves. A few minutes later, four enemy soldiers came out of another bunker that had been bypassed and surrendered. Some of the North Koreans were carrying United Nations safe-conduct passes in their hands. During this final assault, other enemy soldiers were bugging out of the hill. The knoll was secure by 1600. Company G had incurred slightly over 30 casualties, most of which were due to minor grenade wounds. Several other casualties were sustained by the mortar-men as a result of enemy counter mortar fire.'

Right: Five UN senior officers pose with Gen Ridgway in front of the helicopter that will take them to the peace talks at Kaesong, 11 July 1951. L to r: Rear-Adm Burke, Maj-Gen Craigie, Maj-Gen Paik Sun Yup, Vice-Adm Joy, Gen Ridgway, Maj-Gen Hodges
UN (from US Air Force)

The static war

The first anniversary of the outbreak of the Korean War came during the period when both sides were busy establishing defensive lines opposite one another. For a further two years the war dragged on, but it had radically altered in that it was now a mainly static conflict with neither side altering its positions to any great degree. Fighting was mainly defensive in nature, but this did not make it any the less severe for the soldiers involved and the casualties on both sides mounted steadily. UN policy was now to establish a really strong defensive line at the same time as pressing ahead with the agonisingly slow peace talks. From time to time there would be outbreaks of savage fighting, with one side or the other trying to take a particular feature. It must have seemed to many of the soldiers that this was a situation that would last for ever. And, as one might have expected, the vast majority of the public back home lost interest in the war.

There are many aspects of this period which need to be covered, first and foremost the tricky art of living 'in the line'. Next comes the business of patrolling, vital if one is to keep on top of the enemy in trench warfare as any veteran of World War 1 will remember. This is also a good place to cover casualties and that now renowned Korean medical unit the MASH (Mobile Army Surgical Hospital), while a word or two on 'R&R', the NAAFI and PX will not go amiss. To close this section is an account of the battle fought by the Duke of Wellington's Regiment on the Hook in May 1953, which was the last major engagement fought by a unit of the British Army since the end of World War II.

Below: Men of 3rd Infantry Division enjoy coffee and doughnuts during Operation 'Dirt Remover', 11 December 1952. *US Army*

Propaganda

Many POW's like to play chess.

Demand Peace — Stop The War

安全通行證
통행증
SAFE CONDUCT PASS

Headquarters, Korean People's Army
Headquarters, Chinese People's Volunteers

Both sides used propaganda during the Korean War. Much of this effort was directed outside the actual battle area and towards the rest of the world, in order to try to gain support from uncommitted countries, or, by swaying world opinion, to put pressure on the other side, in order to gain an advantage. This was particularly the case during the long drawn out peace talks. However, active propaganda was also directed against the soldiers fighting on the battlefield. This mainly took the form of leaflets, both sides dropping them on the other by means of aircraft, artillery and mortar shells, etc.

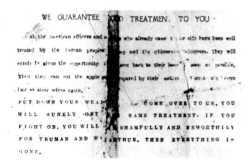

WE GUARANTEE GOOD TREATMENT TO YOU

All the American officers and men who already came to our side have been well treated by the Korean people's army and the chinese volunteers. They will surely be given the opportunity to get back to their homes as soon as possible. Then they can eat the apple pie prepared by their mother and sit down fair with their wives again.

PUT DOWN YOUR WEAPONS AND COME OVER TO US. YOU WILL SURELY GET THE SAME TREATMENT. IF YOU FIGHT ON, YOU WILL DIE SHAMFULLY AND UNWORTHILY FOR TRUMAN AND MACARTHUR. THEN EVERYTHING IS GONE.

SAFE CONDUCT PASS

통행증
通行證

The BEARER, regardless of his military rank or nationality, is hereby unconditionally guaranteed freedom from personal injury, maltreatment or abuse. He will receive medical treatment if necessary and may retain all personal possessions.

ISSUED BY
THE KOREAN PEOPLE'S ARMY
THE CHINESE PEOPLE'S
VOLUNTEER FORCES
KG

No More Fear of Death in Bloody Actions

But Easy and Healthy Life

Scenes from U.S.-British P.O.W's Life in North Korea

104

Left: Both sides of a Communist safe conduct pass, signed by both the North Korean and Chinese commanders. Pass kindly supplied by Lt-Col A. J. Barker. *Adam Forty*

Far left: North Korean safe conduct pass (both sides). *IWM*

Right: UN propaganda leaflet, showing Stalin holding an unfortunate (and unwilling) Chinaman in front of UN guns. *Adam Forty*

Below left: Chinese leaflet on the theme of how nice life was as a PoW. *Adam Forty*

Below: A propaganda leaflet *Peace News. Adam Forty*

Below right: Two GIs of the 23rd Infantry Regt, 2nd Infantry Division, hold a propaganda poster showing American soldiers being driven into the sea. *US Army*

Overleaf: Men of 1st Battalion PPCLI hold Chinese propaganda signs. *Public Archives Canada*

Peace

Immediate Truce Again Offered By China

U.S. Prepares Korean War Extension

War to Spread

+ Job For You, Soldier?

Life in the line

What was it like in the average US infantry company during the last winter of the war? In *Truce Tent and Fighting Front*, there is a good description of the life of the men of I Company, 35th Infantry Regiment, 25th Infantry Division. They were located with the remainder of their battalion about six miles north-east of Ch'orwon, manning the main line of resistance* positions. I Company were in the centre, on a 1,500-yard front, from the broad valley floor to the crest of the north-south ridge more than 100m above the valley. All three pla-

* Main line of resistance (MLR), ie Forward defence localities (FDL) in British parlance.

toons were needed to cover this very broad front, so only Company HQ and mortar crews were located on the reverse slopes of the hilly part of the front, and thus had to assume the role of counter-attack force, normally assigned to the support platoon. To the north of their positions, the 130th Regiment, 44th Division of the CCF 15th Army opposed them, occupying higher ground and thus enjoying excellent observation of the company positions, especially those located on the valley floor. At the eastern end of the company positions, in the hilly area, the Chinese were only 500 yards away, but even at this close range they were difficult to detect, most of their positions being on the reverse slopes with carefully camouflaged openings on the forward slopes for weapons and observation. I Company then consisted of six officers, 174 enlisted men and 49 KATUSAs (Korean Augmentation to the US Army, ie Koreans who were asigned to serve with US Army units). They were commanded by 1-Lt Travis J. Duerr. He was one of the few officers with combat experience and had been in command since October 1952. One officer and 13 men were Negro, 10 Puerto Rican, one

Below: An excellent view of frontline positions, belonging to Company F, 2nd Battalion, 7th Infantry Regiment, US 3rd Infantry Division. The soldiers are eating their Thanksgiving dinner, November 1952.
US Army

native Irish and one native Hawaiian. The KATUSA personnel were distributed along the front line, using the 'buddy' system — each was assigned to an American buddy who was responsible for teaching him some English, care of weapons and other training. Unfortunately the language barrier really prevented them from becoming firm friends, so the attitude was more paternal and in some cases rather patronising.

The company had 39 bunkers, 34 with automatic weapons in them and five which were used as living quarters only. Many of the fighting bunkers were divided into fighting and living quarters housing from two to seven men. Most of the bunker was underground and could be entered from the trench system which linked the complete sector of the front. The bunkers had roofs constructed of thick logs and sandbags, with a burster layer on top composed of loose sand, stones and sticks as protection from artillery and mortar fire. Due to the positioning of the bunkers on the steep, uneven terrain, some of the automatic weapons had limited fields of fire. However, because of the length of its front, I Company had been issued with additional automatic weapons so that they could cover all the possible enemy approach route. One .50cal, six .30cal; heavy and 12 .30cal light machine guns were backed up

Far left, top: A rifleman and a BAR man pour fire down the forward slope of a hill on the western front as snow falls, 25 February 1952. *US Army*

Far left, bottom: 'Chow-time' in the front line. Men of Company F, 2nd Battalion, 7th Infantry Regiment, enjoy their Thanksgiving Day dinner, November 1952. *US Army*

Left: Korean labourers work on a bunker for the CO of the 2nd Battalion, 23rd Infantry Regiment, 2nd Infantry Division near Kumhwa, 8 January 1952. *US Army*

Below: A good view of a typical living bunker used by men of 1st Marine Division. *US Marine*

by 15 Browning Automatic Rifles in the bunkers. In addition, there were three 57mm recoiless rifles, three 3.5in rocket launchers and two M2 flame throwers in open emplacements. The .50cal, five of the heavy .30s and six of the light machine guns, were sited with interlocking arcs of fire ('bands of fire' in US parlance), these were sector weapons and would be left in situ when the company moved on. Were the position attacked then these extra weapons would provide a 'sheet of steel' in front of I Company. Three M4 Sherman tanks, with 76mm guns, from the regimental tank company had firing positions on the ridge line and on the reverse slopes around the centre of the company position, to provide the main anti-tank defence. To back up the company's 60mm mortars were the 60mm mortars of L Coy, the 81mm mortars of M Coy, the 4.2in mortars of the 27th Infantry Regiment and the 105mm howitzers of the 64th Artillery Regiment could be called upon for direct support.

From one to four double aprons of barbed wire had been laid to guard the approaches to the company positions and, in addition, Lt Duerr had erected bands of triple concertina wire in front of and behind the aprons, for increased protection. On each of the four most likely Chinese approaches was a combat outpost, consisting of four two-man foxholes dug in a diamond shape with the point toward the north. Around each post were double aprons of barbed wire, concertina wire, mines and trip flares. By night the posts were manned by three relief teams of an NCO, two riflemen and an automatic team of two men. They stayed put when attacked and fought until ordered back. As most of his men were young and inexperienced, Lt Duerr made them carry M1 rifles instead of carbines, because the M1 clip held less ammunition than the carbine clip, thus ammunition was not shot off so rapidly in a firefight. He had found by experience that those unaccustomed to action had the tendency to fire off all their ammunition in the first few minutes of an engagement — a 'fatal tendency', as he put it! Each platoon had two snipers with rifles equipped with telescopic sights. Duerr ensured that all weapons were test fired every day and that they were stripped and cleaned daily as well, so that they would be ready to meet an enemy attack.

Next to his personal weapon the most important item to the front line soldier was his armoured vest. The men of I Coy preferred the Marine-type vest, which fitted more comfortably and appeared to offer better protection than the US Army issue.

The Marine vest was sleeveless, had nylon padding around the upper chest and shoulders, and had plates of Fibreglass bonded with resin that covered the lower chest, back and abdomen. The Army vest relied upon layers of basket-weave nylon to take the impact of shell splinters. Neither vest would stop a bullet at close range, but could help to decrease the number of casualties from mortar or shell fragments. The men of I Coy were in general agreement that the vests had saved lives on many occasions. Other favoured items of equipment were the mountain sleeping bag and the rubber combat boot known as the 'Micky Mouse'. This sort of equipment provided much needed protection against the rigours of the Korean winter during which a cup of hot tea or coffee would freeze solid if not drunk quickly.

Every night the three rifle companies of the 3rd Battalion, 35th Infantry sent out patrols. These were planned by the regimental CO and his staff and details sent out a day in advance, giving the sector, route, objective, mission, strength, time of departure and special equipment to be taken. The battalion commander often briefed the patrol commander personally on important missions. Companies furnished patrols on a rotational basis, one providing the combat patrol while the other two produced screening patrols — the former probed over 1,000 yards in front of the MLR, while the latter seldom

Above: A soldier of Company G of the Dutch Battalion, assigned to the US 2nd Infantry Division, firing a BAR against the enemy in the 'T-Bone' Hill sector, 18 December 1952. *US Army*

Left: Men move around the trenches outside a machine gun emplacement on the snow covered western front.
US Army

Below: A platoon of 1st RCR relieves a platoon of the 2nd Battalion in the area of the more southerly Hill 187, 20 May 1952.
Public Archives Canada

Above: 1-Lt Don S. Brimball, Company C 6th Tank Battalion, 24th US Infantry Division, crouches behind the turret of his M26 tank after giving the order to fire at Song Sil-li, 10 January 1952.
US Army via Patton Museum

went more than 500 yards. No soldiers went on patrol until they had been in the line at least 10 days. For the rest of the time a soldier would serve as a guard in the trenches, man a fighting bunker or a combat outpost at night, hack trenches out of the frozen ground, or erect tactical wire on the slopes. 50% of the men were always on the alert so two men shared one sleeping bag to discourage shirking! Over 80% of the company's work was at night.

Living conditions were very reminiscent of the Western Front in World War 1 and personal comfort depended a great deal on an individual's own initiative. Men constructed double and triple bunks out of logs, steel pickets and telephone wire, to make the most of the cramped living conditions in the bunkers (usually under 5ft × 8ft). Plastic battery bags served as windows, straw mats covered the dirt floors and candles were normally used for lighting. Oil drip stoves were the 'norm' although charcoal and wood stoves, sunk into the earth, were also used to keep the ground warm. Breakfast and dinner were usually hot meals and served in two mess areas in the company lines, while the midday meal was from C rations. Hot food in marmite (insulated) cans were carried in the company jeep from the kitchen to the mess areas. I Coy had 20 personnel from the Korean Service Corps attached and

they were used to perform all kitchen duties (well known in the US Army as 'KP' — Kitchen Police). Each man had a shower at least every five days to make sure that he kept himself clean. Men were taken in batches to the battalion shower point and received a complete change of clean clothes after showering. Socks had to be changed daily in order to prevent trench foot, while the company aidmen inspected all the men's feet daily as well. Bunkers were sprayed with disinfectant every month and rat poison spread to control that problem.*

The biggest morale booster among the men of I Company was the rotation system, but there were several other ways in which the soldiers were given a change of scene and a chance to relax, albeit briefly. The simplest of these was the 'warm-up' bunker just behind the lines, which served as a place to read and write letters, wash clothes and get haircuts. Normally each man had the opportunity of spending several hours there every three or four days. Each day 10 men left for the Regi-

* Korean rats were a very tough and hardy breed (they had to be!) and sensibly sought the relative comfort of the soldiers' 'Hutchies' as the dugouts were universally called. I remember waking up in the small hours to find one calmly sitting on the end of my bed eating my underwear!

Above: A British forward position, c1952. *IWM*

mental Service Company area — some distance in rear of the MLR — for a complete 24-hour rest period. Finally, during a tour of duty every man could generally expect to be granted one five-day 'R&R' leave in Japan. The initials stood for 'Rest and Relaxation', but as already mentioned they were universally known as 'Rack & Ruin' for obvious reasons. When an I Company soldier approached the magical mark of 36 points which qualified him for rotation 'Stateside', he usually stopped going out on patrol — mainly because the man in question tended to become over cautious and less dependable, thus putting the rest of the patrol at risk. Rotation of units and sub-units on the MLR was clearly good for morale and took place at every level from platoon up to corps level, so the survival chances of the individual were good during this static period. However, it had some bad effects as well. The lack of enemy air operations made everyone careless about the use of camouflage and far too much material and supplies were collected around ports, depots, etc. The presence of the Korean Service Corps was also a mixed blessing as it relieved combat soldiers of the boring chores, inevitably making some of them soft and spoilt. Finally, the static war encouraged everyone to collect far too much kit. Units and individuals surrounded themselves with masses of surplus clothing and equipment, which could never have been moved in unit transport — for example, it took one US artillery battalion in 7th Infantry Division, three full days to move its unit and personal gear from one sector to another!

A day in the line

This account of a day in the line in Korea was written by Lt V. S. C. Tyndale, 4th/7th Royal Dragoon Guards, while he was serving with the 1st Royal Tank Regiment and appears by kind permission of RHQ RTR and CO 1 RTR:

' "Wake up sir, it's three o'clock. Time to get up, sir." The troop leader yawned and stretched, then hastily slipped his arms inside the bedroll as the cold night air licked them. "Righto, Kemberry, I'll be out in a few minutes. Would you please light the candle" — then, as the other did so and left, "Thanks."

'The quivering flame of the candle lit the inside of the hutchie — a square hole carved deep into the side of a Korean hill. It was just long enough for a bedroll, and two feet wider. Within reach of the occupant was a drip-fed fire, consisting of an ammunition box, a fuel pipe leading to it, and a chimney of 20pdr ammunition cases rising from it up through the roof. In a quick movement I reached over, flicked the tap on and dropped a match in the flash pan. After a few moments of luxurious last minute rest, the air inside lost some of its fierce bite and I put my outer clothes on. Combat jacket and windproof trousers were followed by a balaclava, three pairs of gloves, another pair of socks, a furry hat and a parka. Switching off the petrol and blowing out the candle to avoid the ever present danger of fire, I stepped outside and stood still for a few minutes to let my eyes become accustomed to the darkness. It was a clear moonlight night, with an icy wind blowing hard from the north. Everything seemed still, though there was an angry grumble from artillery in the distance, and an occasional stacatto burst from harassing machine guns. To my left I could hear the steady hum from the charging engine of my tank. I moved quietly towards it and was challenged by a figure from the shadows. "Halt! Goal," it hissed. I stopped abruptly and whispered "Post", the current password. "OK sir, everything is pretty quiet." "Off you go then. Good night." "Good night sir." I slipped into the weapon pit and looked down into the valley. My gloved hands ran over the Bren and I checked that the magazine was full. There were several boxes of grenades and I made sure that these were primed. Some which were resting on the ground had to be prised free from the earth, frozen hard since they were moved earlier in the night.

'The tanks of the troop were dug deep in pits, in the right hand side of the largest hill of the area, Point 355. This was known by our American allies as Little Gibraltar, or "Hell Hill". Looking back over my right shoulder, I could see my own tank just a few yards away, its bulk partly hidden by the pit. The generator had been switched off, but the high pitched buzz of the wireless set was audible. The wireless crackled as a message came over it, and I heard my own operator answering a routine call. I saw a movement a little way away and, as a figure approached, challenged him. It was the relief who would be with me until dawn. I beckoned to him to take first shift in the turret and he disappeared inside. When he was satisfied with the wireless and everything else, he dismissed the previous sentry and his head and shoulders reappeared in the hatch as he joined me in keeping observation, in the meantime checking the operation of the Browning machine gun mounted atop the turret. We stared out into the re-entrant below, which ran down into the valley, scrutinising each shadow carefully, for the Chinaman is an excellent patroller. We faced north and the wind cut into my exposed parts. The hood of the parka was moulded into the position from which one could see most and expose least. Peering out into the dark, however, one's eyes soon

Below: Men of the Black Watch use a .30 Browning against Chinese positions. *IWM*

watered from the freezing wind and after a while they would play strange tricks. One night my fellow sentry tiptoed over and whispered he could see a bear. To my right a heavy machine gun opened up and the tracers appeared from behind a hill, soared gracefully, and disappeared as they burnt out, each in the same place, like a chorus appearing, gliding across the stage, and disappearing as abruptly as they had come. A few seconds later the sound would reach me, and then the tracers would reappear, sound and sight alternating. As my feet became cold I stamped them and kicked against the side of the pit. Although wearing two pairs of socks and the the "cold wet winter" boots issued by the Army, with plastic insoles inside them, and standing on straw to insulate my feet from the frozen ground, the icy cold had still seeped through and was creeping into my toes. One wriggled one's toes all the time while standing and this slowed up the freezing process. I glanced at my watch and found that I had done my turn in the pit, and so took over the set from the operator, who climbed out. Within the turret the lower part of one's body was out of the wind at any rate, and gradually recovered, but all too soon it was time to emerge again.

A Vickers machine gun opened up on my left, from higher up the hill, and this

Above: Men of 3 RAR improve their defences. *IWM*

Right: C Squadron, 1 RTR command post. *George Forty*

Below right: Author's dugout on Point 121. *George Forty*

time the tracers put me in mind of the lit-up hoardings that one used to see in London, publishing the news abroad to all and sundry. Soon these became fainter and harder to see as the east became lighter. Once more I was privileged to see a beautiful dawn break in *Chosen* — "The Land of Morning Calm". When it was really light we stood down, handing over the 24-hour wireless watch to another tank. Those who had just come off guard slept while the others prepared breakfast. When this was ready I ate it eagerly, for the fresh air had given me an appetite. This morning it consisted of a tin of ham and heated Lima beans, and an egg with some bread. I found the ham in the last mouthful of beans and it tasted excellent. A thick brew of tea soon restored my spirits and I went outside to boil some ice for washing. Last night it had not snowed, but everything was frozen and the previous fall of snow lay hard. A little later in the morning I walked over to see my right-hand tank, about a quarter of a mile along the front. My troop was in support of the Australians, and I saw the Diggers doing various jobs as I passed, or sleeping after patrol, or simply chaffing one another in their usual good-humoured manner. My troop sergeant's tank was supporting the 1st ROK Capitol Division, and I entered a company area of theirs. I had quickly acquired an admiration for these plucky determined little fighters, and they in turn were very appreciative of tank support. During the night a Korean patrol had located a mortar position and, having reported it, this tank of mine was destroying it. When we achieved direct hits, followed by secondary explosions, the ROK delight knew no bounds, and they bounced up and down clapping their hands in glee and shouting "Number One!" — an expression denoting great pleasure. I found the

crew in great heart and we chatted for a time, while they pointed out new diggings and recounted anything of local significance which had taken place during the night. Walking back to my tank I found some Diggers sitting round passing the time of day with my crew. As a general rule the Australians were a little older and more self-reliant than our fellows, although often their platoon commanders were young. I could not have served with better soldiers.

'In the meantime the other members of my crew had been keeping the front under

Above: Diggers laying protective wire in front of their positions.
Australian War Memorial

Far left, top: An 'Elephant House' position for a Centurion on Yong Dong. *George Forty*

Far left, bottom: Squadron C, 1 RTR Centurion ARV (suitably inscribed) comes to the rescue of a broken down Centurion. *George Forty*

Above left: A Centurion, minus track, being pulled up the side of Point 121. *George Forty*

Above: Men of 1 RAR thaw out in the wintry sunshine in front of their bunker. *Australian War Memorial*

observation, and one of them had spotted a wireless aerial. I computed the range on my map and opened fire on it. We hit it, snapping it in two, but evidently it was near some headquarters, for a few days later it had been erected again. The inevitable followed and it once more disappeared. Leaving observers, we made our way down to the cookhouse of "Dog" Coy and there had a hot lunch cooked from fresh rations. As I walked back a shell screamed overhead and buried itself in the ground beyond me, throwing up a heap of earth and sending shrapnel singing by. I dived into a nearby trench and awaited the next. The arrival of shells is sudden and surprising; something like the emotional impact of being in a passenger train when an express with its steam whistle screaming hurtles past in the opposite direction. If one can hear the whistle one is soon able to tell a "comer" which is going to be a near one, from one that is going to drop a hundred yards away and one takes precautions accordingly. Listening for the next, I heard it coming in a little nearer the tank and, as it landed, I sprinted to the next cover; and so by leaps and bounds reached the tank itself and hopped inside, closing the cupola lid as something landed nearby, then started sending back an accurate report on this incoming fire. Having sent this report, we opened up on all known enemy observation posts, seeking to silence the guns by discomforting the OP crews. The most effective way of doing this was to put a shell into each slit, in the manner of posting a letter. This we did, and the shelling became desultory and finally ceased.

As evening drew on, the local company commander informed me of the coming night patrols, and as I could be of practical assistance in one I chatted with the patrol commander, a young Australian officer, and we planned effective support. Before last light I ranged on a particular supply trench that the Chinese used at night to bring up rice and ammunition, and also on one spot to which the patrol hoped to lure the enemy. We carried out this ranging in the middle of a general "shooting-up" of trenches, positions, OPs etc, in order that the enemy might suspect nothing. Then as the sun set, we stood to. While dinner was cooking we fired intermittently at the supply trench, breaking up the intervals between shots and occasionally firing two or three in quick succession to harass those bringing up supplies. Then I handed over to one of my crew while I ate. As the patrol in which I was particularly interested was not going out until nine o'clock, I lay down for an hour's rest, while the other tank

carried on the harassing. I wrote out the day's events and then relaxed. I was soon asleep. My rest, however, was to be short-lived, for I was woken abruptly by a shell landing close by, and shaking dirt from the roof on to my face. As more and more came in, landing methodically round us, it was obvious that they were gunning for the tanks again. I went outside and instinctively ducked as an "in-swinger" hailed its approach. Without waiting for its partner, I hopped into the tank. As it was nearly nine anyway, we stood by to await the patrol, the while listening to the wireless net on which we were operating. More shells followed and a jarring crash accompanied by fumes told us that we had received a direct hit. I took a quick look round to see whether there was any serious damage and, finding none, hopped in and continued to listen. The shelling eased up and we opened the cupola lid to have better observation. All seemed quiet, then down in the valley below a burst from and Owen gun preceded a fusilade of firing in which one could distinguish the fast chattering "Burp gun" of the Chinese. Little flashes appeared and the sound of grenades exploding was carried to us, and cries — perhaps of pain or fear — were audible. Then silence, followed again by an outburst of firing. All at once the deep cough of enemy mortars was heard and — ages later, it seemed — the flash of them landing, followed by the familiar crump. A few minutes of silence followed and I was beginning to wonder whether the patrol commander's set had been damaged when a message crackled over the air, electrifying us by its urgency. "Hullo Buck Rogers Dog One-Nine, Starlight One Zero Now, Over." I answered "One-Nine Wilco Out" and before I had finished the first round had been fired by the gunner, who was ready for this. A few hectic and strenuous moments followed as one round after another sped on its way. When we had fired them, I reported so over the wireless and the cryptic message came back: "One Nine, successful. Thanks Out." The trap had been sprung! By now the moon was up and the patrol made good time back, reporting in at a quarter to eleven. As the guard alternated each night, I and my fellows were to come on at twelve, so we left the tank and went to bed. As I lay down to sleep I heard the tank engines starting up, to prevent it freezing but nothing could stop me and I was soon asleep. Another day in the line was over.

On the other side of the hill

An excellent description on the way the enemy lived is given in the Canadian official war history, *Strange Battleground*, by a Canadian soldier, Cpl J. J. A. Pelletier of C Coy 3rd Royal Canadian Regiment and is reproduced by kind permission of the Ministry of Supply and Services, Canada. Pelletier was captured after he had been wounded during an enemy attack on his company position on the night 2-3 May 1952, one of the last major actions of the war involving Canadian troops. He was taken across the valley by a group of 30 Chinese, half of whom were carrying wounded on their backs. Having crossed 'No man's Land' they climbed half-way up the enemy held hills, where they entered the Chinese tunnels:

... They walked about 12 yards in, then climbed down a 10ft ladder, then made their way along a twisted corridor. Both passages and rooms led off the main corridor. Finally the group of prisoners ... was halted on one of the off-shoot passageways. The prisoners were searched and books, wallets etc removed. The Chinese did not take watches or rings and returned wallets with money intact. The prisoners remained in the passageway an hour or more and were then taken outside again. As they left the "honeycomb" by a different route, the Corporal lost his orientation and cannot locate the route followed. All he knows is they took him to another hill and another honeycomb. Including the route to the first honeycomb, the Corporal estimated he moved through about 700 yards of enemy trench. "Trench" is actually the wrong word; it varied in depth from two to six feet and shelling had so pounded the positions that it was more of a gully. There were no fire bays, but every 20 yards or so along the trench there was a Chinaman standing to. Behind him and in the side of the trench was a three-foot hole. This hole may have been an entrance to the honeycomb or merely a shelter from our shelling. All the Chinamen were armed with burp guns.* The Corporal never saw any enemy carrying a rifle. He saw one machine gun set up and that was at the enemy forming-up places near the base of the C Company positions. The entrance to the second honeycomb was again like that of a mine but this time it was located almost at the top of the feature. The tunnel extended for

10 yards, then there was a 10ft ladder down, then a tunnel for about 25 yards, then another ladder, then another tunnel and yet another ladder. All the tunnels slanted downwards and by the time the Corporal got to the main part of the honeycomb he thought there was as least 100ft of overhead cover. While the Corporal was in the position, it was bombarded by our guns (or mortars?). Only the faintest tremor was felt within the honeycomb and the sound was like that of a man drumming his fingers on the table.

'The tunnels or passageways and the rooms were shored with beams again as in a mine. Where the beams did not cross the walls were bare earth. Overhead, there was a continuous roof of logs three to four inches in diameter. To a greater extent than the first honeycomb, the second was a mass of offshoot passageways and rooms. The passageways were only 5ft high and the rooms were sometimes only 3-4ft high. The main room looked like a briefing room and was about 20ft square, but again only 5ft high. The walls were canvas lined and there were goat and sheep skins on the floor. In this main room there was a rack of weapons where the Chinese could deposit their guns when they entered and pick them up when they left. The Corporal saw five of our Brens, and some of our rifles. But the Chinese never took these weapons with them when they went out. They carried only burp guns. Also armed with burp guns were the women. These were dressed as the men, wore long hair and seemed to be regular soldiers. The Corporal was not certain about ammunition supply. At various places he saw piles of stuff covered with rice mats and believed this might have been ammunition. He did not think food was under the mats because bags of potatoes and rice were left uncovered. The honeycomb was dry and clean (the Chinese removed their shoes at the entrance), well ventilated (by holes to the outside some two feet in diameter) and not smelly (bodily wastes were deposited in the paper tube containers for mortar bombs and these disposed of in some fashion). The place swarmed with Chinamen and the Corporal thinks he saw up to 500 in the second homeycomb. The Chinese treated him with more curiosity than animosity. Most of the time the Corporal lay in one of the little sleeping rooms. When he opened his eyes he would find many of the enemy looking at him through the doorway, as if he were an animal in a zoo. Then he would close his eyes and that group would go away, but when he opened his eyes again there would be as many Chinamen as before ...

*The Chinese SMG or 'burp' gun, so named after its characteristic high rate of fire, was probably the Russian PPS-41, Pistolet-Pulemet Shpagina o 1941 g, five million of which were made during World War 2 alone! Another possibility was the later version, the PPS 43, also 7.62mm, which was rushed into production by the Chinese during the Korean War with a 35-round magazine and an effective range of some 100m.

Patrolling

The UN Command decision to stop limited objective attacks in the spring of 1952, so as to allow the peace negotiations to be resumed at Panmunjon, meant that the Eighth Army could only keep contact with the enemy by patrolling and raiding. These had limited effectiveness. Certainly they kept front-line troops alert and gave them valuable combat experience, but they did not often produce much useful information, few prisoners were taken and on some occasions no contact whatsoever was made. In April 1952 most regiments at the front sent out at least one patrol and several ambushes every night, rotating the roster between battalions. Patrolling was always one of the most dangerous and tricky tasks undertaken, mainly by infantry soldiers, during the static war. Often, sitting in the turret of my Centurion tank, listening on the patrol radio frequency of the battalion I was supporting, I used to imagine what it was like being out in the middle of 'No Man's Land', in the darkness, using one's sense of sight, hearing and smell, more like a wild jungle animal than a civilised human being. I still have my copy of the patrol plan for the 1st

Battalion the Duke of Wellington's Regiment, for the night of 16/17 May 1953. It shows that a total of some nine standing patrols, one protection, one ambush and one recce patrol were sent out that night. My tanks, the battalion mortars and medium machine guns, plus the guns of the supporting artillery battery, were all ready· and waiting to give fire support to these patrols. we normally used a system of pre-arranged and plotted DF (Defensive Fire) tasks. Each evening when we brought the tank up into its firing pit, we would carefully position it in exactly the same place, using marker posts to show where the tracks should be, then the gun would be traversed on to another pair of 'in line' marker posts. We then zeroed the traverse indicator and measured all our night DF tasks as switches from the zero line. Having registered them all in daylight, we were able to bring down fire with pinpoint accuracy in the pitch dark and in a matter of seconds. We would wait, for example, on tenterhooks for one of the highly vulnerable standing patrols on the normal enemy lines of advance to the Hook feature, to reply to control's whispered query as to whether they were still OK. 'Blow once into your mike if the enemy are close, twice if all is OK,' would be the whispered command and we would wait, hardly daring to breathe in case we missed their barely audible reply. Sometimes all was well, but on many occasions, a burst of small arms fire in the darkness would herald the order to fire a particular DF in order to cover the patrol's hurried return to the main defensive line.

To illustrate this important feature of the static war are two stories. The first

Below: Leathernecks of 1st Marine Division in the Wonju-Hoengsong area, check the houses in a Korean village. *US Marine Corps*

concerns a night patrol carried out by men of Company K, 15th Infantry Regiment, of 3rd Infantry Division, as told in *Truce Tent and Fighting Front:*

'The 15th Infantry, commanded by Col William T. Moore, occupied a sector south-west of Ch'orwon and west on Yonch'on. Company K, under 1-Lt Sylvanus Smith, was responsible for a piece of the front about eight miles west of Yonch'on, just to the west of the big double horseshoe bend of the Imjin River. In this area the terrain was made up of small hills flanked by flat valleys covered with rice paddies. Since the patrol mission was to bring back prisoners, the choice of objectives was extremely limited. The Chinese maintained only three positions within patrolling distance of Company K and the routes to these were well known to both sides. As it turned out, the 3rd Battalion commander, Lt-Col Gene R. Welch, selected a position manned by what appeared to be a Chinese reinforced rifle platoon, located about 1,500m north of the main line of resistance. On a boot-shaped hill, called Italy, some 150m high, the enemy outpost kept watch over the activities of the 3rd Division units to the south. 500m to the east of Italy across a broad rice valley with a meandering stream lay Greece, a many ridged hill that resembled the Greek peninsula in its outline. Lt Smith drew up the patrol plan and had it approved at battalion and regimental level. It visualised two rifle platoons reinforced by a machine gun section from Company M moving out in three groups during the evening toward Italy. The security group, composed of the MG section and a rifle squad, would take its position on Hill 128, overlooking the valley between Italy and Greece. One rifle platoon, serving as a base of fire group, would move forward to Italy and halt 350m from the Chinese outpost. Once the base of fire group got into position, the assault platoon would pass through and attack the outpost from the south-west. Each group would have a telephone (EE-8) and a radio (SCR-300) to maintain contact with the others and with battalion in case it became necessary to request aid or the laying down of pre-planned artillery fire along the patrol route. The handles were removed from the phones to eliminate the ringing and noise that might betray the patrol's position and the instruments were to be spliced into the assault line running forward from the MLR. Flare signals were arranged but not used during the patrol. To provide preparation fire, two batteries of 155mm guns and one battery of 105mm howitzers would fire for five minutes after the base of

fire group got into position on Italy. Two 105mm would continue to fire until the assault group was ready to attack the objective.

'Since the patrol was to be conducted at night, the riflemen selected to go on the mission were given intensive training in night fire techniques. Using battery-operated lights to simulate enemy fire, the riflemen were taught to aim low and take advantage of ricochets. Sand-table models of the patrol route and objective were carefully studied and the patrol leaders flown over the whole area to familiarise themselves with the terrain. Since most of the personnel already had been over the ground on several occasions, the members of the patrol were thoroughly briefed by the evening of 16 April. They were also informed that a regimental patrol would set up an ambush on Greece that night. The majority of the rifleman carried M1 rifles with about 140 rounds of ammunition and two or three hand grenades apiece. The LMGs in the base of fire group were provided with 1,000 rounds of ammunition and the crews also carried carbines. Each man wore a protective nylon vest against shell fragments. In the security group heavy machine guns were substituted for light at the last moment, since they were to be used in a fixed support mission and the heavier mount would give more accurate overhead and indirect fire.*

'A hard rain had turned the ground into a sea of mud on 16 April and the night was dark, chilly and windy with temperatures in the mid-50s. At 2100 hours the security group under Lt Smith led the way through the barbed wire and minefields fronting the company positions. Next came the assault group, led by M/Sgt George Curry, composed of 26 men of the 2nd Platoon with three aidmen and two communications men from Coy HQ. The base of fire group, under 2nd Lt John A. Sherzer, the patrol leader, completed the column as it sloshed through the muck down into the valley below. Sherzer had 26 men from his own 1st Platoon, one aidman and two communications men. There were also 12 Korean litter bearers accompanying the assault and base of fire groups in the event of casualties. Smith's security force had no trouble as they climbed Hill 128 and emplaced their machine guns. But a sudden explosion from the minefield in front of the company positions soon halted

* The .30 calibre US machine gun M1919 was the standard air cooled version, used as an infantry squad weapon with bipod, butt and carrying handle, whilst the M1917A1 was the water cooled version and the standard support weapon.

the assault group. Sgts Frederick O. Brown and William Upton went back to investigate and discovered that one of the medics and a Korean litter bearer had started late. Losing their way in the dark, they had wandered into the minefield and tripped a mine. Fortunately the mine had fallen forward into an old foxhole, so the blast had carried away from the two men, who were unharmed. Brown located the approximate spot where the mine had exploded and notified Battalion HQ to rescue the men. By the time Brown and Upton joined the waiting patrol, half an hour had been lost. As the assault group resumed its advance and rounded the shoulder of Hill 128, another element of delay entered the picture. From the 1st Battalion sector off to the right, flares went off lighting up the valley leading to Greece and Italy. Every time a flare illuminated the sky, the patrol hit the ground and waited until the glare subsided. Pleas back to the battalion to have the flares stopped were unsuccessful. The snail-like pace of

the patrol was further slowed by the practice of halting the groups in place whenever a burnt-out cluster of huts were encountered. Cpl William Chilwuist, in charge of the lead squad, checked the huts along the route that had to be reconnoitered, so it was well after 2300 hours by the time the patrol reached the last burnt-out settlement close to the foot of Italy. Since the assault platoon now had to cross a broad stretch of open ground to get to the selected approach ridge to Italy, the base of fire group set up four LMGs along the bank of the small stream traversing the valley. With Chilquist's squad leading, Sgt Curry's force moved in single file across the exposed area along the top of an earthen paddy dike where the footing was less sloppy. At three yard intervals, the members of the platoon then began to climb to the first small rise on Italy. As the lead elements reached the spot, a few seconds of quiet, and then the chatter of a burp gun shattered the night. From the lower reaches of Greece, machine and rifle

Above: A patrol of 5th RCT, 24 Infantry Division, advances toward Chinese positions, past a dead enemy soldier. Note that the left hand man is carrying a British Bren LMG. *US Army*

fire swiftly followed as the Chinese sprang their ambush. Evidently the enemy had set their trap along the north-south valley between Italy and Greece, expecting the patrol to approach their outpost by this route which had been used by the Americans in the past many times. Only the fact that the ridge rather than the valley had been chosen as the access path prevented greater catastrophe.

'The initial enemy burst tore through the assault patrol and hit four men. A rifle bullet pierced the protective vest of Pfc John L. Masnari, one of the BAR men and ripped into his chest. Mortally wounded, he told his buddies not to bother about applying first aid, moaned slightly, asked for a priest, and then died a few minutes later. He was the first man to be killed in Korea wearing body armour. The other three men took wounds in the head, arm and leg — painful but not critical injuries. After the shock of the Chinese onslaught wore off, the assault platoon became angry and opened up with every available weapon on the enemy. Sgt Curry tried to inform the other groups and battalion of his situation by phone, but the instrument did not work. The radio was of no assistance either, since the aerial had been put out of action by a Chinese slug. For the moment the assault platoon was completely as its own. Back at Battalion HQ, Col Welch knew that something had gone wrong, but refused to lay on artillery fire until the patrol's location could be pinpointed; otherwise he might shell his own men. The base of fire group, in the meantime, took cover when the enemy opened up by jumping into a hip deep stream, since there were no fences or rocks and only one tree to crouch behind. One of the machine gunners was caught by an enemy burst of fire and took four or five bullets in his leg — the only casualty in Sherzer's platoon. For 10 minutes the two engaged platoons from Company K exchanged brisk fire with the Chinese, then the enemy force withdrew. Curry's force, with four casualties, no communications, very little ammunition left, and the element of surprise gone, decided to pull back and rejoin Sherzer's group. Since the Korean litter bearers had dropped their loads and headed back toward UNC lines at the outbreak of the fight, Curry's platoon had to carry its own dead and wounded. Using M1s and field jackets, the men fashioned supplementary makeshift litters and started back down the hill; there was no further enemy fire.

'Shortly after midnight, the two platoons combined forces and communications with HQ were re-established. The flares from

the 1st Battalion were still going off, despite the urgent pleas of Sgt Brown to ''get the damned flares out''. This meant that the patrol and its wounded had to drop or be dropped quickly each time a flare dissipated the darkness. Not only did this delay the return of the patrol, but the rough handling also made the trip very painful for the wounded. The men of the base of fire platoon, in addition, were wet and chilly from their stay in the stream. Nevertheless, the combined group inched their way back towards Company L's position, where they would get litters through the barbed wire obstacles with less difficulty. At 0330 hours the weary patrol crept into 3rd Battalion lines and gratefully gulped down the hot coffee and doughnuts that awaited them. Meanwhile the regimental ambush party set up on Greece had moved forward and covered the area used by the Chinese to ambush Company K's patrol; they found no signs of the enemy. In the morning, however, a battalion raiding party discovered a bloody cap and number of bloody bandages on Greece, indicating that the 8,000 rounds of ammunition fired by the patrol had found some targets — the patrol estimated that the enemy suffered five killed and 20 wounded in the fight.'

This then was but one of the hundreds of patrols sent out and its part failure should be balanced against the often successful ones, such as the following short description of a daylight raid by 1st Battalion the Duke of Wellington's Regiment, which was reported by Maj Hugh Pond MC, a military observer in Korea, and is included here by kind permission of RHQ the Duke of Wellington's Regiment:

Above: Lt Hatcher M. James and five men of a Raider Company, attached to the 9th RCT, 2nd Division, after returning from a seven mile patrol into Communist lines, north of Sabangu on the central front. The burp gun was taken for a North Korean who was one of four killed in a moonlight fire fight. All the raiders returned safely. *US Army*

' ''During the period a raiding party of two officers and 15 men carried out a successful raid.'' That is how the action by 1 DWR was recorded in the divisional operational summary, but this is the whole story. Several jeeps pulled up in the dark at a forward jeep head, just behind the frontline, and several dim figures alighted and gathered together. The patrol directing officers had arrived, and led by the CO, Lt-Col F. R. St P. Bunbury DSO, they strode off, silhouetted for a moment on the skyline and then swallowed up in the darkness. The group walked at a steady pace along a meandering, rutted track, between mine and paddy fields. The night was still and frosty, stars twinkled brilliantly overhead. There were few sounds of war only an occasional artillery shell or a burst of small arms fire. Not so very far ahead, a bored machine gunner, warming his weapon, tapped out ''How's your father? — Alright.'' then silence again. A slight noise of clanking weapons, a muffled cough and then out of the darkness came the 17 men who were going on the raiding party. They passed in silence except for one Yorkshire lad who muttered to a chum ''Ee lad, the officers are up early this morning.'' Shortly afterwards a truck and an ambulance jeep passed, lights out, at a steady pace.

'At a casualty clearing post, behind one of the forward companies, from a sandbagged jeep shelter, a young officer cheerfully served out hot tea to the patrol. The skyline in the east gradually lightened. and soon one saw the mud-covered faces and equipment-laden men — young men who not so many months ago were working in the mines, factories and shops at home, and who have exchanged span-ners for bayonets, picks for rifles and footballs for grenades. As the light became brighter and the time drew near for the patrol to leave, officers and NCOs checked the weapons and made sure that no identifying papers were being carried. The men reluctantly handed over treasured letters and photographs. A sergeant suspicious of one man said: ''Come on now, I bet you've some beer hidden away somewhere,'' ''No Sarge'' came the reply, ''but I've got an opener in case we find any over there''. A final check, watches synchronised and the Colonel gave the order to move off. They filed down a valley carefully spaced out, walking confidently, weapons at the ready, and disappeared round a hill towards a gap in the minefield. The CO and his control officers moved up the hill into the warren of dugouts and trenches of this infantry company. Camouflage nets cover the tops of the communicating sandbagged trenches, and stairs are made from dirt filled ammunition boxes. Thin black pillars of smoke issue from pipes sticking out of mounds which cover the tops of sleeping and living quarters. The men who had been told to stay under cover, in case the enemy shelled the area, sat in the doorways of the ''Hoochies'', smoking, drinking tea, waiting for the guns to start. The object of this daylight raid, briefly, was for the men to go out and blow up a newly built emplacement. For about a fortnight beforehand, eagle eyed watchers from observation posts had seen activity in a certain area. Men carrying logs, sandbags and tools. Through binoculars the watchers had got to know the workmen so well that they had given them names: ''Wong'' for the little stocky chap;

"Kong" for the fat white clothed man, and "Song" who seemed to be in charge of the work. When the work was nearly complete the CO gave out his orders: "Blow up the work and kill or capture the labourers." Up in the control post, wirelesses switched on and telephones nearby, the Colonel, an Artillery officer and a Tank officer settled down in a narrow dirt slit, and gazed through a wooden visor on to the area of attack. At eight o'clock precisely, the divisional artillery roared out in unison. From behind came the shock of shells escaping from 25-pounder muzzles, and then the high-pitched whine as the shells hurtled overhead on to the Chinese positions. Dust and rocks hurled into the air and the trenches and camouflage above the observers' heads, trembled with the concussion. After the first salvo, vapour-like trails appeared in the sky and plunged to the ground, giving off smoke to cover the advance across open ground. Purple streaks shot across the front as tank gunners sent high explosive rounds into known enemy positions. At last in the middle of No Man's Land valley, the patrol

appeared, a single line of small men, still well spaced, almost jog trotting. The leader paused to test the ice of frozen stream and then crossed. They moved along the bank past a lone shivering poplar tree, across a shell burnt patch of ground, over the crest of a small hill and out of sight.

'The shells and mortars continued with the smoke and explosions, and the valley and opposing hills were soon obscured by the masses of smoke and dust, except for the top of a bomb pocked hill, which jutted from the smoke into the now blue sky. In the control post the officers were receiving information from the patrol leader, details of location and progress. Short sharper orders were given to the gunners and tank crews to change targets or increase fire. So far no enemy retaliation. At 0825 hours message received: "On the objective." 0826 hours: "Assault party moving forward." 0830 hours: "Assaulting now." Ears strained to catch the sound of small arms fire in between shell burst, but nothing was heard. The next wireless message; "Emplacement blown, no prisoners, all occupants blown to bits, we have one dead Chinaman, shall we return?" The Colonel ordered them to come quickly and to bring the dead man with them. The fire plan continued and the smokescreen kept thickened. A few enemy mortar bombs began to land in the area, but they were scattered and ineffective. The officers returned to the casualty clearing post to await the return of the patrol. Eagerly men poked heads from the bunkers to ask how it went, and were told as much as possible. They grinned thankfully and passed it on to friends inside.

'The group waited impatiently by the jeep ambulance, which, with luck, would not be used except for the dead enemy. The artillery became desultory and finally almost stopped. The crump of a few mortars landing in the valley alerted them and as the sound got closer they spread out ready to take cover. Then on the skyline appeared two figures moving swiftly, and following behind them a group carrying a stretcher. The patrol had returned. Several men detached themselves from the group and ran to assist with the burden. Sweating and tired but all smiles. One grinning man shouted: "Where's that photographer? Tell him that Errol Flynn is back." (A *Pathe News* cameraman filmed the patrol.) They were urged into the waiting truck, which took them back, along a camouflaged road to the comparative safety of a reserve company. Tea was waiting for them, and as they sat and lounged in the dust they told what happened. 2-Lt Ian Orr, who was born in

Birkenhead, told of how the assault party crept up, shrouded in smoke, to the emplacement and heard Chinese talking and coughing. They paused while the main party took up defensive positions and then charged forward. The opening to the dugout was about 6ft by 3ft and seemed to go into the hillside for about 10 yards. Orr threw a phosphorus grenade, which was answered by a burst of fire from a burp gun. No one came out so more smoke and HE grenades were tossed inside. Then the Engineer, Cpl Ieuam Jenkins of Louth, was ordered forward to throw in the explosive charge. They all then dashed away and threw themselves to the ground as the timber supports and rocks shot 40 feet into the air. They were all lifted bodily off the ground and large stones, wood and earth crashed all round them. Sgt Tom Dickie from Druckendult said, "It nearly broke my eardrums and smothered me in dust." Lt Rodney Harms of Knaresborough took up the story. He commanded the main party: "We heard a scuffling in a nearby trench and saw a Chink. One of the lads fired, but missed, I threw a grenade which knocked him over." Pte Brian Hastie of Goole, who helped carry the dead man back said: "He was very heavy and certainly made us sweat." Cpl Andrew McKenzie of South Shields, reckoned that the dead man was more like a Mongolian than a Chinese. Others said that his uniform was smart and clean and looked quite new. He was later identified as a Chinese officer. The divisional commander and the bridgadier both came round while the CO was talking to the men. They listened with interest and congratulated the men on a job well done. Lt Col Bunbury said afterwards: "The patrol was very nearly 100% successful, and the thing that pleases me is that they all came back without a scratch. They did a fine job." '

Top left: Maj-Gen Mike West, second GOC 1st Commonwealth Division, talking to men of 1 DWR after their return from patrol. *RHQ DWR*

Bottom left: Men of 1 DWR on their return from blowing up the Chinese bunker — note the cosh and mixture of Stens and Owen guns. *RHQ DWR*

Above: Led by Lt Rodney Harms the main party of the Dukes daring daylight raid comes back into friendly territory. *RHQ DWR*

MASH

'This is a comedy that's brave enough to recognise that people get hurt in war, and base its comic vision on the idea that brutality is to be hated. There are people shooting at one another and if you try to stop them they'll shoot at you. The ugly fact of being imprisoned in a madhouse like that drives them funny'*. That is how the actor, writer and director, Alan Alda, described the amazingly successful comedy series M*A*S*H, which has already been running for over eight years in the USA (and six in UK). A phenomenally successful and consistently popular television programme, it has been shown all over the world, has been sold to 60 different countries and dubbed in more than half a dozen languages — the only place they don't seem to be able to sell it is in Korea!

The average Mobile Army Surgical Hospital, was a well equipped military hospital of about 60 beds, 11 doctors and some 100 personnel in total. It was the first medical unit in the chain of evacuation where major surgery could be performed

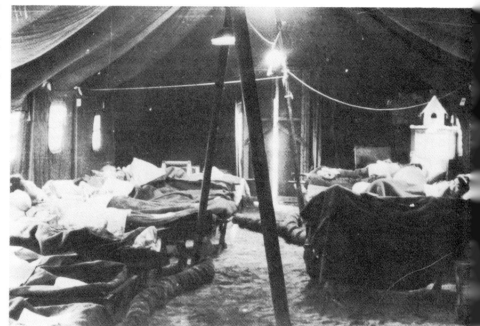

* Quoted from the *Listener* of 17 January 1980.

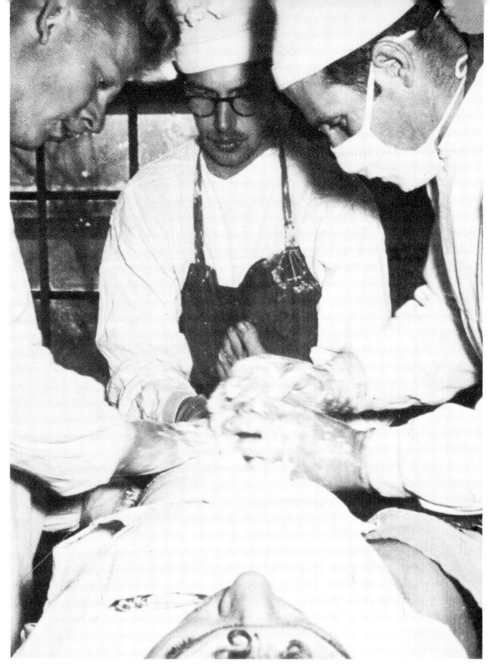

Top left: Headquarters of the Norwegian MASH.
Dr Odd Oyen

Centre left: Postoperative ward NorMASH.
Dr Odd Oyen

Far left, bottom: 60 Independent Indian Field Ambulance. *F. E. Smith*

Bottom left: The Swedish hospital, Pusan.
Swedish Embassy, London

Right: Putting a leg in plaster.
Swedish Embassy, London

(the chain being: battalion aid post — casualty clearing station — MASH — rear lines medical unit — base hospital in Japan — home). A MASH kept patients until they were stabilised after their operation, which normally took a few days. They were then fit for transportation to a rear hospital where surgical treatment could be completed. One such MASH was the Norwegian one (NorMASH) which was incorporated into the medical services of the Eighth Army in May 1951 and went on functioning well after the armistice was signed, until November 1954. It represented the Norwegian contribution to the United Nations forces in Korea. India provided a field ambulance, Italy and Sweden each provided a field hospital, Denmark a hospital ship and a medical team.

NorMASH was administered initially by the Norwegian Red Cross until 1 November 1951, when the Surgeon General took over on behalf of the Norwegian Defence Department. All members of the hospital were volunteers, the majority coming from the reserve, with few regulars. Their service in Korea, surprisingly, did not replace their normal compulsory military service. Personnel were engaged for six months, but out of the 632 Norwegians who served with the MASH, over 100 stayed on voluntarily for longer than a year. The NorMASH also had some American and Koreans on its staff, while there were, during its three years in existence, a total of 111 female nurses, in addition to the 22 male nurses, 80 doctors, five dentists, six pharmacists, seven chaplains and 392 other staff. None of the

Norwegians was killed in action, but two were killed in an accident. The hospital treated, wherever possible, civilians as well as military personnel, and this became even more the case after the truce. As well as 'in-patients' NorMASH treated large numbers of soldiers and civilians as out-patients, also serving them with food and coffee whenever they could manage it. Altogether the NorMASH treated over 90,000 patients (14,755 in-patients), the largest group being Americans, South Korean and British Commonwealth soldiers; however, almost all those countries whose troops fought in the UN Command, were given treatment at some time or another. For most of the static war period the NorMASH was located at Tongduchonni, just north of the 38th Parallel, and served the British Commonwealth Division, quickly establishing a marvellous rapport with all units.

One of the doctors with the NorMASH in Korea, Dr Odd Oyer, wrote about those days:

'Almost none of the personnel who served in NorMASH had any previous experience in that type of unit. The surgeons, anaesthetists, nurses and all the rest were well educated in their jobs on a peacetime basis, and some had taken part in World War 2, but in different jobs. The time they spent at NorMASH was an unforgettable experience for a variety of reasons. First of all everyone was tested to the utmost to use their skill to do the very best for the wounded under fairly primitive conditions. Secondly, we quickly learned that a hospital must be a friendly place as well as a medical institution if it is going to really help the wounded. Last but by no means least, we became great friends with the men of the very different nations that went to make up the Commonwealth Division. Such fine units and yet so different in many ways. The wild "Vingt Douze" (the nickname of the Royal 22nd Regiment) from Canada, the New Zealanders, the Australians and the British themselves were all really something. Medical activity of course depended upon the intensity of the fighting, quiet periods with only a few wounded changed quickly to very active periods when our resources were stretched almost to breaking point. On such days and nights the value of proper registration and effective examination and sorting became apparent.

'The units for shock treatment, X-Ray and the operating theatre with four operating tables, worked around the clock almost to a point of complete exhaustion. For example, at one time in 1953, 173 operations were performed in a 72-hour period.

It was vital during such periods that some of the professional personnel be rested, so as to prevent all of us becoming exhausted at the same time. During such periods, non-medical personnel were put on to assist during operations and did a fine job. After an operation we usually kept patients for about three days but sometimes they stayed longer. The consumption of blood was enormous. The medical practice at that time was blood for blood lost (it was before the Ringer wave) and not much electrolytes. All blood was given as Rhesus Negative, Type O, without crossmatching. And every bottle was tapped in USA, transported to Japan and from there to Korea. 30 transfusions for one wounded man was not unusual. Typical wounds were shrapnel and mine casualties, and the lower extremities suffered most. Legs crushed up to the knee was a tragic event. Because of splinters most casualties had multiple wounds. All central nervous system damage and eye injuries were taken by helicopter to specialised units further behind the front.

'NorMASH was from the beginning placed in the Commonwealth Divisional area, and we quickly developed a good understanding with the soldiers of the division. This good relationship showed in the tremendous hospitality given to those from NorMASH visiting units and vice versa. Our chaplains served as welfare officers and played an important role in representing the MASH to other units, and arranged entertainment for the patients and staff, for example, by inviting bands like the Black Watch pipers and so on. For all the patients it was a great morale boost to be nursed by female nurses. Combatant officers said that they felt the morale of units was higher when they knew that there were female nurses behind their positions.

'I still correspond regularly all over the world with friends I made in Korea. For example, the son of one friend who was the padre of a New Zealand battalion, is now studying for a doctorate in Norway. A seargeant who died in the NorMASH was buried at the war cemetery in Pusan, and the senior chaplain of NorMASH not only still corresponds with his family, but has also been to visit the grave and to lay a wreath in 1962 and again in 1971. This sort of experience reflects — even stresses, what we find in peacetime — the importance of the human attitude in a hospital. It must be said, however, that the film M*A*S*H does not quite cover the reality of life at NorMASH. The whole business was, literally speaking, too bloody.

The PX and the NAAFI

The PX and the NAAFI

The PX (Post Exchange) is the American equivalent of the British NAAFI (Navy Army and Air Force Institutes); it is the place where the soldier can obtain some of the comforts and necessities of civilised life, such as cigarettes, toilet articles, sweets, etc. The part that the PX and the NAAFI played in boosting morale in Korea cannot be overemphasised and so both excellent organisations justly deserve their place in this book. The PX was first on the scene and less than a month after the first UN troops had landed in Korea, PX supplies were being unloaded at Pusan. Headed by two officers, a volunteer staff of civilians from the JCE (Japan Central Exchange) landed with that initial shipment of supplies and proceeded to establish the first JCE distribution points in Korea less than a month after the fighting started. Tobacco, beer, snack items and candy were in greatest demand and a distribution chain was quickly established to get them up to the combat zone. Train, truck, barge, aircraft and even LST were used. In the absence of drinkable water there was a great demand for soft drinks and ice cream. (Many of those who were new arrivals at Pusan docks will remember the very large notices which read 'To the Coca-Cola Plant'.) Mobile PXs were used as well as static distribution points, as evidenced in the following quote from the *Japan Exchange* magazine of January 1955:

'Our fleet of 10 new mobile post exchanges with Yuletide cargo rolled up to front-line divisions in Korea early in October giving US fighting men in action their first opportunity to Christmas shop. The gaily-decorated touring PXs gave quick on the spot sales service to troops off duty from their front line action for a few hours rest and relaxation. The rolling exchanges went into operation early to ensure adequate time for Christmas orders to be delivered to their US destinations. A wide range of carefully selected merchandise samples gave shopping servicemen a choice of many gifts for wives, families and friends back home. Such luxury items as electric roasters, electric blankets, typewriters,

silver and jewellery were included among many other items . . . After 15 November, the 10 Christmas-order buses were restocked with regular PX merchandise and were routed with eight regularly scheduled mobile PXs to division and corps service. The new mobile PX service brings merchandise to our troops operating within sight of enemy lines. Acclaimed a powerful aid in bolstering the morale of our fighting forces, the new mobile PX frontline service will continue on a year round basis.'

As well as truck-mounted 'mobiles' there was a two-car PX train and even a C-47 Air Force PX! The Pusan depot had some difficult problems to overcome which related to security, transportation and personnel. A constant 24-hour surveillance

Below: Purchasing supplies in the Post Exchange Car at the Taegu Railroad Yards, 425th Traffic Regulating Group, US Eighth Army, 2 February 1952. *US Army*

Bottom: American and ROK troops of the 5th Regiment Combat Team, purchase hard to get items from a mobile PX near Kusong, 31 October 1950. *US Army*

was necessary to prevent stealing from unloading barges and even from the warehouses. Interestingly, as far as transportation was concerned, PX supplies rated second only to munitions and other top priority material, while capable, able-bodied male labourers were very hard to find as most of them were already serving in the ROK Army, consequently many women had to be employed.

In Britain, the NAAFI had asked for 200 volunteers to run their operations in Korea and were swamped with applications from as far away as Aden. It was remarkable that while female staff were difficult to get for service in bases in England, more than enough volunteered for the danger and discomfort on the Far Eastern battlefield. This discomfort was to prove even worse than that experienced in World War 2. The cart tracks, which formed the majority of roads outside the main towns, were unsuitable for heavy traffic, becoming rivers of mud in the winter and clogged with dust clouds

Above: Sgt Ed W. Presley purchases a carton of cigarettes at the GHQ Long Lines Signal Group PX, Pusan, 31 March 1951. *US Army*

Left: The PX must get through! A Browning LMG team provides defence for a railcar mobile exchange, February 1952.
HQ Army and Air Force Exchange Service

Right: NAAFI in Korea.
George Forty

NAAFI in KOREA

(Top): A shot taken from the verandah of Naafi's "North-lands" Roadhouse. A tank going forward to the battle front is at odds with the gay garden sunshade in the foreground.
(Centre): A helicopter view of the "Newcastle" Roadhouse.
(Bottom): This picture of "Northlands" shows the thatched roof and attractive architecture, features common to all of these famous and popular rendezvous.

NAAFI, the official canteen organisation for H.M. Forces at home and abroad, in peace and war, is proud to have served shoulder-to-shoulder with the men of the Commonwealth Forces in Korea—and proud to continue that service to those who have returned to the U.K.

NAAFI canteens, clubs, grocery shops, sports shops, wines and spirits supplies for Messes, special caterings for reunions and other celebrations, and specialist printing of die-stamped stationery and greetings cards represent a few of the hundred-and-one activities in which Naafi is engaged exclusively for British sailors, soldiers and airmen everywhere.

NAAFI

THE OFFICIAL CANTEEN ORGANISATION FOR HER MAJESTY'S FORCES

Imperial Court, Kennington Lane, London, S.E. 11   Telephone: RELiance 1200

131

in the summer. All water needed chemical treatment and in the winter even hot tea froze if it was put on the ground! There were no buildings in the wilds that could be taken over as canteens, so the NAAFI had to build their own using timber and mud walls and rice straw thatched roofs. The resulting wayside roadhouses were the pride of the British Commonwealth Division and the envy of everyone else. They received their supplies by helicopter at times and served the troops in the firing line by lorry. The NAAFI history 'Service to the Services' recalls that some of their drivers were intrepid to the point of recklessness. One drove blithely into the middle of a tank battle and had to be shunted to cover in order to shield him and his precious cargo from the enemy. Much of the NAAFI's stock came from Japan and Hong Kong and there was a similar gift service to the one already explained for the PX. NAAFI staff had to resist the temptation to give food or clothing away to the local people, because when they did they were immediately inundated with beggars. However, they did, as their history points out, indirectly contribute to local housing — many Koreans built themselves shacks out of discarded NAAFI crates and beer barrels. Even empty beer bottles became part of the local currency!

Above: Men of Headquarters 2nd Battalion, 7th Infantry Regiment, 3rd Infantry Division, receive PX.

Right: Another view of the Seoul PX.
HQ Army and Air Force Exchange Service

Below right: The *Ship Inn* NAAFI roadhouse was only about three miles behind the line. *George Forty*

´R+R´ and living in Korea

Above left: Taking advantage of a lull in the battle to play a game of cards, near Sin Hung-Dong, are these men of 38th Infantry Regiment, 2nd Infantry Division, 2 April 1951. *US Army*

Above: Men of the 7th RCT, 3rd Infantry Division, read their mail and relax at a rest area south of Seoul, 3 May 1951. *US Army*

Left: Maj Robert Botright prepares to leave the 2nd Infantry Division airstrip to drop C-rations to men of the division at the front, 25 September 1951. *US Army*

Above right: This captured
Russian built truck was
remodelled to run on the rails,
December 1950.
UN (from US Army)

Right: Bob and Diane Scott,
members of a USO troupe sing
a duet for men of the 2nd US
Infantry Division at the
Bulldozer Bowl. *US Army*

Below: 'The Rice Paddy
Daddies' of 2nd Infantry
Division get together for a jam
session, after the day's work is
done at the 2nd Replacement
Depot, 22 May 1951.
US Army

Top: One of many famous film personalities to visit Korea was Errol Flynn, seen here with a group of American and Commonwealth NCOs. F. E. Smith said that Flynn made a big impact on all those he came into contact with. *F. E. Smith*

Above left: Part of the Dutch Battalion enjoy a singsong during their training in winter 1950-51. They had not yet received US clothing and wear British battledress. *Royal Netherlands Embassy, London*

Above: Officers of 1 DWR follow their CO (Lt-Col Bunbury) during a night party while the battalion was in reserve. *Lt-Col A. J. Barker*

Left: Australian soldiers give sweets to children in Seoul. *Australian War Memorial*

135

Right: Canadians playing hockey at the 'Imjin Gardens', 4 February 1952. Teal Bridge can be seen in the background. *Public Archives Canada*

Below: Men of 3rd Recce Company, 3rd Infantry Division, play volleyball after evening chow, while in reserve at Yongdongpo, 11 May 1951. *US Army*

Bottom: Men of 1st Battalion Duke of Wellington's Regiment attend an open air Church Service. *RHQ DWR*

Top left: RASC ration lorries load up (and sample the goods!). *Soldier*

Top right: Not corned beef again! An RASC corporal of 29 Brigade checks a load of corned beef on to his lorry. *Soldier*

Above left: Entrance to the Commonwealth Division Rest Centre in Korea. *IWM*

Above: Street scene in Hiroshima gives a good impression of the fascinating things to be seen while on R&R in Japan. *George Forty*

Left: A 'must' for all tourists to Hiroshima was the Atomic Centre, Ground Zero for the atomic bomb dropped at 0815 hours on 6 August 1945. *George Forty*

The Bloody Hook

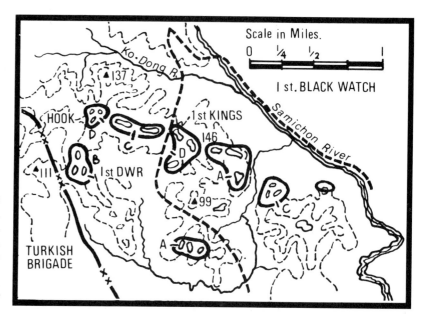

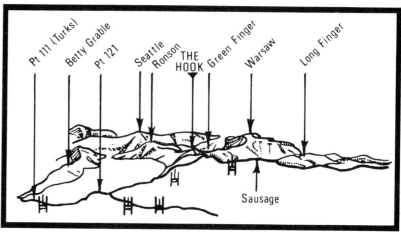

On 18 May 1953, a small unarmed Chinese soldier, by the name of Private Hua Hong, of the 2nd Battalion, 399th Regiment CCF, became one of the most important people in Korea, at least to the men of the Commonwealth Division, when he walked, smiling, into the forward positions of C Company of the 1st Battalion, the Duke of Wellington's Regiment (1 DWR), and surrendered. He was fed up with the war he told them and had information which he knew would be of interest. Without any form of coercion, apart from a mug of tea and a cigarette, he willingly imparted the important news which an army of intelligence officers had been trying to obtain for weeks. His information was that the Chinese were about to mount a heavy attack on the positions of the 'Dukes' with a first wave of five companies and a follow up echelon of a further three. Unfortunately the most vital piece of information, namely the date of the attack, was missing, but had plenty of details about everything else.

Above: The Battle of the Hook, May 1953.

Left: Hook trenches in the snow. *Lt-Col A. J. Barker*

Above: Panorama of the Hook from Warsaw. *IWM*

The target for this attack, was the feature held by the Dukes which rejoiced in the code-name of 'The Hook'. It was one of the main features dominating any approach from the north via the Samichon valley and it had already been the scene of some bitterly fought battles during the current hostilities. Two of these are well remembered. The first was fought on the night of 26/27 October by the 7th United States Marines when, under the most unfavourable conditions, they captured the Hook, then lost it and then recaptured it again, losing over 200 men in the process. The second, and a costly battle in numbers of Chinese casualties, took place on the night of 18/19 November 1952, when the 1st Battalion, the Black Watch, beat off all comers to retain their positions. The Black Watch were again holding the Hook when the final battle of the Hook began on the night of 7/8 May with a strong probe, and ended with a three-battalion attack against 1 DWR on the night of 28/29 May. This final bloody battle was the last major

action to have been fought by a British battalion this century. It was a protracted and drawn out affair, as the enemy built up its mortaring and shelling to a crescendo, while the defence sought to maintain the initiative by active patrolling. This was coupled with continually building up the strength of their defensive positions, by wiring, mining, tunnelling and all the other aspects of trench warfare. The battle came to a climax on the night of 28/29 May 1952, when a greater concentration of artillery was brought to bear on a 100-yard front than at any time since the end of World War 1.

The Dukes, mainly composed of young National Servicemen from the West Riding of Yorkshire, suffered heavy casualties, but held their positions in the face of odds of five to one against them. Two DSOs, six Military Crosses and Military Medals were awarded to the defenders. One of the DSOs was awarded to the Dukes' Battalion commander, Lt-Col Ramsay St Pierre Bunbury DSO, the other to Maj Lewis Kershaw, and

I have been fortunate enough to persuade Lewis Kershaw to put down some of his recollections of the battle. He is an ideal person to begin with and to describe the battle area and the build-up period:

'Viewing the terrain looking north from the Hook the approach past it is readily seen by virtue of a wide valley some three quarters of a mile wide, flanked by the Hook on the south-west side and Point 146 on the north-west. This was known as the Samichon valley and had been used by Ghengis Khan in the 12th century, who swept through towards southern Asia. This time it was to prove the stepping point for another ambitious horde. As you traverse the view further, there are many hills and valleys, the hills seldom rising more than 200 feet high, but it was the blind side of the hills which proved most help to the enemy, because he could shelter large numbers of assault troops there, with little hope of us being able to shell or mortar them even when we discovered a build-up was taking place. The only way to find out what was happening was by regular patrolling, building up a comprehensive picture from their reports. The situation over a period of some two weeks before 28 May, had begun to show clearly that the Hook was once more to be the brunt of another attempted enemy break through of our lines. The preceding days had seen an intensification of enemy patrolling and probing all along the battalion front. Shelling and mortaring had been gradually increasing, reaching a crescendo on 27/28 May. Many enemy had been observed moving into large bunkers opposite our immediate front.'

Left: My tank in its layback area, when I was occupying the position in the saddle between the Hook and 'Sausage'. Note the .50 Browning on its 'ad hoc' mounting. *George Forty*

Prior to 27 May, Lewis Kershaw had been in charge of the erection of protective wire in front of the Hook positions. Night after night he had personally supervised this hazardous operation, working often in bright moonlight very close to the enemy, who mortared the working parties constantly. This work was a major factor in defeating the enemy, as it was afterwards proved beyond doubt that the main assault was held up and finally broken on the wire erected under his guidance. Lewis Kershaw goes on:

'On the 27th at dusk, I had moved up to the Hook from our battalion HQ position, some 500 yards to the rear, with my batman and a radio set. My duty was to relay from the Hook to Battalion HQ, messages I received from a small patrol composed of one officer and one NCO, whom we had previously sent out to lie up in No Man's Land and report on all enemy movement. Our messages were sent at pre-arranged times, so that undue wireless traffic could be avoided which might have aroused the enemy's suspicions. Reception was good until the late afternoon and evening of the 28th. My last message relayed to Battalion HQ was about 1800hrs.* At this time I was in the forward platoon HQ of the Hook company. The platoon commander (Lt Ernest Kirk) was receiving his final briefing from his company commander, some 100 yards to the rear of the Hook. I had his section commanders and platoon sergeant with me, awaiting his return. By now the shelling and mortaring had considerably increased and I was worried about his return, as most of his journey would be in open trenches, eventually leading to his platoon command post which was underground. Lt Kirk returned at about 1830, after in his own words: "A mad dash to get under cover". He at once started issuing his orders to his section commanders. The tempo of shelling and mortaring was increasing rapidly and I was worried about the stability of the platoon HQ command post, as large pieces of the earth roof were showering down on us. Finally Lt Kirk told them to return to their posts with all speed.'

At 1953, when it was still broad daylight, the enemy suddenly brought down a tremendous concentration of artillery and mortar fire on to the Hook, Point 121 and the Sausage feature. This included fire from self-propelled guns, firing indirect, but controlled from enemy forward OPs, which destroyed or neutralised all the

---

* Capt Colin Glen and Cpl Duncan 'Spud' Taylor who formed the patrol had gone out during the night of 26 May, to lie up near a small bush about a mile below 'Green Finger' (see map). All day on the 27th they lay hidden in a small hollow, radioing back their reports every two hours. Mostly these were 'nothing to report', but as darkness came again Chinese activity increased, and parties of men passed close by their hideout. They had to spend another full night and day in their exposed position, until they were able to send their final message: 'This is it!!' as the Chinese platoons raced past them. They could do nothing more than only to wait in their lonely hideout until the battle was decided. Eventually on the 29th they started to make their way back, but got caught in a minefield where Capt Glen was killed. Cpl Taylor was picked up by a Kings' patrol, dazed but alive.

automatic weapons along the front of the forward platoon of the Hook. Within a few minutes of the bombardment the enemy attacked from the direction of Green Finger, throwing grenades and satchel charges into the weapon slits as they assaulted. At this stage the forward platoon commander was killed in hand to hand fighting and co-ordinated platoon action became impossible. Typical of the individual section actions fought by the men of the leading company was that of Cpl John Walker's section. He was visiting his fighting bunkers when they came under intense enemy artillery fire. He then tried to get a message back on the radio in his section command post, but the wireless set was now buried under the debris of a direct hit. Returning to his section bunkers, he found they were untenable as all had received direct hits and, realising that he was now unable to hold the forward positions, he rallied his men and ordered them to withdraw to a nearby tunnel. Cpl Walker remained behind to cover their withdrawal, engaging with this Sten gun six enemy who rushed his position through the damaged slit of a fighting bunker. He then found that three or four more Chinese had jumped into the trench behind him and were advancing towards his section trying to cut them off. Cpl Walker threw grenades at them and climbing out of his bunker, covered his section back, stage by stage into the tunnel. Once in the tunnel he organised its defence and then tried to break out of the other end, but found his way blocked by another party of enemy. He personally fought them with grenades until the roof of the tunnel collapsed, sealing the exit. Returning to the other end he made another attempt to sally forth, but came under heavy machine gun fire and was forced back. For the rest of the night Cpl Walker and his men fought a tenacious defensive battle in the tunnel while the enemy tried their hardest to dislodge them, twice calling upon them to lay down their arms and surrender, but they held out until dawn. Cpl Walker was awarded the Military Medal for his leadership and personal courage.

Successive waves of enemy attackers suffered very heavy casualties and were prevented from reaching the positions or evacuating their own casualties, because of the weight of the retaliatory fire, which included both the Corps and Divisional artillery, firing at all known enemy gun and mortar positions, likely forming up points, reinforcement routes, HQs and control posts. The same procedure was repeated as each successive wave was located. While the battle was in progress,

three separate waves of enemy, each approximately 30 strong, were seen approaching from Ronson. They were scattered by artillery and tank fire from Point 121 and LMG fire from the left hand platoon of the Hook company. At 2030 the enemy fire lifted on to the jeephead and shortly afterwards a large number of Chinese were seen on the crest of the Hook, held up by the wire. Heavy casualties were inflicted by VT* and LMG fire and no further advance was made. Of the troops who attacked the Hook, one complete company coming from the northwest was almost completely wiped out. This was substantiated from intelligence sources which reported that the reserve company had to clear the battlefield as all the assault company were either killer or wounded. The reserve company however, suffered so badly that they in turn could not evacuate the casualties.

At 2045 a second attack was launched from the Warsaw-Long Finger direction against the right hand platoon and the tank in its immediate vicinity. The tank engaged and drove off a large body of the enemy on the wire, but had its searchlight shot out by burp gunfire. Other groups of enemy, in the

Above: Parachute flares cast an eerie glow, during a night battle on the Hook position.
George Forty

* VT — a proximity fuse contains a built-in radio transmitter/receiver which transmits a continuous wave during flight. As the missile gets nearer the target a reflected wave is received. This latter wave interferes with the former and produced a signal which increases in volume as the distance decreases. When a certain voltage is attained the signal is used to fire an electric igniter, thus exploding the shell before it actually strikes the target and producing a lethal 'rain' of shell fragments on the enemy troops in the open.

Left: Mortar pit and ammunition bunker on the Hook. *Maj L. Kershaw*

Below: An artist's reconstruction of one of the tunnel encounters between men of the Dukes and the Chinese, which appeared in the August 1953 edition of *Soldier* magazine and is reproduced here with the Editor's kind permission. *Adam Forty*

meantime, had penetrated the platoon positions and fighting took place in the trenches and bunkers. The platoon was reinforced and further penetration was prevented. One enemy company was to follow through after the Hook battle finished, but was caught by the DF and had heavy casualties. A planned counter-attack by elements of 1 DWR subsequently restored the situation. Intelligence sources later said that a third attack, comprising an enemy force of two companies, moved towards Point 121 at about 2200, but suffered such heavy casualties from artillery fire that by 2240 they were given permission to withdraw leaving at least 34 killed. A fourth and final attack was mounted by the enemy in battalion strength about 2305 moving towards Point 146 (held by 1 Kings). They were caught in the open and suffered very heavy casualties, needing extra help to clear the battlefield. Meanwhile a reserve company of 1 Kings had relieved B Coy 1 DWR on Pt 121 and the Dukes company was then used to reinforce the Hook Company. At 0030 the enemy attacked again, this time from the Betty Grable direction, south of Ronson ridge. In the flares and searchlight they presented an excellent target for the assault pioneer platoon and the tank on Pt 121, who with artillery and mortar support broke up the attack. Next morning over 30 bodies were counted on the wire.

The restoration of the Hook position, the only one the enemy had penetrated on the battalion front, went ahead steadily from 2300, and by 0430 the Hook was reported completely clear of enemy. Shortly

afterwards the Yong Dong tanks saw large numbers of the enemy moving across the valley from Paris, and the tank on Pt 121 saw a lot of movement on Seattle but by this time the enemy was doing his best to get clear of the battlefield. An immediate engineer recce of the Hook company positions revealed that all principal bunkers of the forward and right hand platoons were damaged and useless for the next two days; the bunkers, some of which were eight feet deep, were in many cases levelled by the intensity of the bombardment; tunnels and the covered trench had withstood the bombardment, but the enemy had blown in the entrances with satchel charges; although the defensive wire was considerably damaged, it was responsible for delaying the enemy and thus preventing him from overrunning the position on the late stages of the attack.

To return to Lewis Kershaw's personal account of the battle. We left him in the forward platoon HQ of the Hook company, sending information back to Battalion HQ from the patrol out in No Man's Land and, very worried about the roof of the dugout falling in:

'My last message had informed Battalion HQ that large numbers of enemy troops had been seen moving into prepared positions in front of the Hook, and I was certain in my own mind that the Hook was about to be attacked again. The roof of the platoon CP was now in obvious danger of collapsing and so I left with my batman to go to the Gunner Observation Post, some 15 yards along an elbow-shaped trench,

Above: Maj R. de la H. Moran, 2IC 1 DWR greeting Gen Maxwell Taylor, CG Eighth Army, during a visit to the battalion in April 1953.

which led to another covered trench housing the two Gunners, responsible for directing our artillery fire support. I then left the OP to find Lt Kirk, as I was not happy about leaving him in his command post, but on the way back I met him and his platoon sergeant, shouting that the CP had finally collapsed completely. The time was now about 1915 and a tremendous amount of shelling was falling on us, as the enemy began dropping into our trench. The platoon sergeant had now climbed down a short ladder which led to a deep underground shelter, capable of holding stores — such as ammunition, water etc, and a number of men (approximately 10). Looking back on this particular time, I realise now that it was true that the Chinese were prepared to accept casualties from their own barrage and, furthermore, would strip a casualty of his weapons. Not all the enemy were armed with rifles, some carried satchel charges and grenades for blowing in our bunkers. The open trench in front of us had all but now collapsed. Lt Kirk and myself were standing side by side, throwing hand grenades at the enemy. We had a buttress to our left behind which we could take cover after we had thrown them. It was whilst Ernest Kirk was leaning forward, throwing another grenade, that he was killed by a burst of fire from a burp gun. He slumped on to my feet, pitching me backwards to the top of the access shaft to the deep under-ground shelter previously mentioned. I scrambled down this ladder and almost immediately a grenade landed behind me — considering

that there was only a space of less than two feet square at the bottom of the ladder, it was a miracle that it landed behind me! I should explain that these Chinese grenades were of the percussion type, and, apart from the small amount of metal in the tin casing and mechanism, relied upon the stunning effect of the blast rather than severe wounding or death. The effect of this one was to blow off my steel helmet and cause me to drop my Sten gun. I knew I had also been hit in the legs and back, as things became rather wet there shortly afterwards. However, I was still mobile and got to the entrance of the stores bunker, where I grabbed a Sten out of the platoon sergeant's hands. It was while firing this up the way I had come that another grenade must have exploded at my feet and toppled me over again. I was then only able to crawl towards the inside of the bunker. Needless to say, there was considerable confusion during all this time and the stores in the bunker had caught on fire. Later both entrances were blown in by the enemy and we were sealed in it until a rescue party arrived at approximately 0600 on 29 May. Apart from seeing the enemy arrive, I had no further view of them up on the surface of the Hook once we were trapped in the deep bunker. I didn't in fact know who was in possession of the Hook, so I asked for a volunteer to go outside the bunker, just before we were rescued, to try to find out the position — you can imagine how we felt when we heard his joyous shouts of: "They're ours!" when he came back. It was whilst lying in the bunker that I realised my right foot was shattered and lying at a drunken angle from the lower part of my leg. I managed to get a tourniquet on my thigh, using a bootlace, which seemed to take ages before I was able to place it at what I thought was in the correct position. I was unable to put a field dressing on my injuries as I couldn't get the plastic covering of the outside of the package. Later one of the others trapped with me managed to do this for me. My journey out of the bunker was rapid, considering the shambles I saw on being dragged out on a ground sheet and later when being placed on to a stretcher jeep at the rear of the Hook. Trenches had collapsed and part of our journey had to be undertaken in full view of the enemy, but a timely smokescreen laid by our Mortar platoon helped considerably in evacuating our dead and wounded. The Hook was still being mortared, but nothing like the previous day... After spending some nine months convalescing I was fitted with an artificial limb and continued to serve for another ten years, certainly much richer in experience and with a sound confidence in the British private soldier, who is more than a match for any future enemy'.

Maj Lewis Kershaw has left out a lot of the details of his horrific night in the bunker — 'It was hell in a four-and-a-half-foot hole' is how one of the nine men sealed in with him explained it later. But for Lewis Kershaw's example one or two might have gone mad. The citation for his DSO gives the full part he played explaining how he had been the last to enter the tunnel and no sooner had he done so than a party of enemy appeared at the entrance and started throwing grenades inside. Maj Kershaw had immediately opened fire with his Sten gun, killing the leading man. He was then wounded seriously by a grenade but, undaunted, continued firing until all his ammunition was gone. Although unable to stand, he then began hurling grenades from the ground, thus preventing the enemy getting into the tunnel. Finding their entrance baulked, the Chinese threw in a petrol bomb, setting fire to the tunnel mouth which they subsequently blew in with high explosive. Meanwhile another party of enemy had destroyed the other end of the tunnel, completely trapping the occupants, some 10 in number in the now pitch darkness (the fire had been put out). Although in severe pain and suffering much loss of blood, Lewis Kershaw took complete control and only after steadying and instilling confidence into his men did he lose consciousness. It goes without saying that, when the morning came, despite his severe wounds, he insisted that all the other wounded should be treated before him and would not be evacuated until he had made a full report to his CO. It was thanks to men like him that the Dukes held the Hook.

The actual layout of the Hook position and of the other company locations is firmly imprinted into my brain, because it was my troop of Centurion tanks, five in all, which was providing them with direct fire support. We had been up there with the Black Watch and remained in position when the two battalions changed over. One tank was on the Hook itself, one in the saddle between the Hook and the feature named Sausage (just to the east), two centrally placed on Point 121 just south-west of the Hook, and finally a fifth tank was west of the Hook, just inside the Turkish sector. My personal part in the final phase of the battle was brief, as I was wounded on the morning of the 28th by a Chinese mortar bomb, while outside my tank, in the act of climbing up to the top of the Hook positions to spot for an indirect fire shoot against an enemy OP which we could not see well enough to engage with direct fire. However, the Centurions played their part in the battle, providing much needed fire support for the hard pressed infantry. John Macfarlane, the troop sergeant, who was commanding the tank in the saddle near the Sausage feature, was largely responsible for breaking up at least one major Chinese attack, for which he was awarded a well-deserved Military Medal. The second troop sergeant, Cpl (Acting Sgt) A. J. G. Wallace, also received an MM for his part in the action. All told the troop fired 504 main gun (20pdr) rounds of HE, 22,500 rounds of Besa and 2,500 rounds from the cupola mounted Brownings. Every tank was hit at least five times by enemy shell and mortar fire, and although all suffered superficial damage all remained in action. Lt Tony Uloth, who had taken the troop over when I was casevac, undoubtedly caused the Chinese a lot of casualties when he engaged the 'Ronson trench' — the mouth of a Chinese tunnel which they had dug to within 15 yards of the Dukes front trenches and which they subsequently used for their assault.

So much for the Hook battle. 'The Dukes held the Hook as I knew they would' said Brigadier Joe Kendrew, commander of 29th Brigade, after the battle. Perhaps the finest compliment to the Commonwealth Division as a whole, was made by the commander of the US Marine Division who occupied the part of the front of the west of the Commonwealth Division boundary when he said: 'You know, I have the sea on my left flank and the Commonwealth Division on my right, and when I go to bed at night I sleep well, because I know that when I wake up in the morning they'll both still be there.'

Below: Farewell parade held just before the Duke of Wellington's left Korea in November 1953. *RHQ DWR*

Prisoners of war

Communist POW camps

'In the POW camps of North Korea are prisoners of many nationalities. Mostly they live in Korean houses in the pleasant villages along the banks of the Yalu River, among some of the most beautiful Korean mountain scenery. There is no barbed wire around the camps. Prisoners are known by their names and not by numbers. Their personal property has not been touched and many have wrist watches, fountain pens and cigarette lighters.

So reads the opening paragraph of an article entitled 'Daily Round,' which appeared in a well illustrated book: *United Nations POWs in Korea*, which was published by the Chinese People's Committee for World Peace, in Peking in 1953. The article continues: 'They retain their own uniforms on capture and in the camps are fitted out twice a year with new summer and winter outfits. Their summer clothes and their winter clothes are warmer than American or British issues. Suitable footwear comes with the seasonal change of clothing. Fuel is ample. The men get more food than is laid down by the Geneva Convention relative to the treatment of Prisoners of War. Special arrangements are made to meet the religious traditions of food for Moslems. A tobacco ration of five ounces is issued weekly. Pipes and cigarette papers are supplied. Camp life in all its aspects is run democratically. POW committees arrange their clubs, messing, sports, recreation and other activities and keep contact with the camp authorities. A description of camp life is provided by Frank Noel, AP photographer who was attached to the US Army when captured. He writes: "The internal functions within the camp are run by the POWs themselves. Camp-wide elections, usually held at 60-day intervals, determine the various committee heads. Elections are by secret ballot. Considering the circumstances, the Chinese have been fair and lenient and provided extra rations and sport facilities over and above the requirements stipulated in the Geneva Convention regarding the rule regulating the conduct and care of prisoners of war. The POWs prepare their own food and have complete run of the large Chinese-type kitchens, bake and steam their own bread and butcher the pigs. Beef is killed by the Chinese, and fish and chicken are brought from nearby China. The Turks are issued lambs, muttons or chicken whenever the day's menu calls for pork. They also prepare their own Turkish-style dishes and can do with their rations whatever they wish according to their taste.

' "Strict cleanliness is not only observed in the kitchen but throughout the camp. All foods are thoroughly cooked and drinking water well boiled before it is set out in the convenient and large crockery jars to cool. A Saturday morning inspection is carried out here regularly. The rooms are emptied of floor mats; bedding aired and the rooms and windows scrubbed and swept clean. Clothing, food utensils and toilet articles are arranged in a neat and set pattern and after the blankets and quilts are aired and shaken out, the room is prepared for the inspection team made up of POWs who are accompanied by a Chinese doctor and a member of the administrative staff. Usually at two-week intervals the Volunteers' medical team gives the room

Below: UN troops recently captured, begin their long march northwards to the PoW camps.
Chinese People's Committee for World Peace

and bedding a good going over with DDT. All POWs have had regular inoculations against typhoid, tetanus and cholera. There is a daily sick call for anyone feeling under the weather or needing checking over. Whatever work the POW does is strictly for himself. The Chinese carpenters and labour gang repair and keep in shape the buildings and the actual construction of the large Oriental style baths. The POWs brought the stones from the nearby streams for enlarging the kitchen and baths which will accommodate at one time the 12 men squads. Wood in regular cut lengths to fit the fire boxes under the kitchen pots is brought here by barge. The POW's unload the barges and pair off and carry the wood stretcher-style. This wood is also used to keep the houses warm during the winter. Church services for both Catholics and Protestants are held in the camps each Sunday. A mobile movie projection team usually manages to show Chinese or Korean-produced movies every two weeks. And almost every Saturday night the dramatic group works up new gags, stunts and skits to put on a good stage show. Borrowed musical instruments help out and the singing quartets all manage to put on a two-hour show. After one of these shows the kitchen crew bring out doughnuts and the simulated coffee. The British take their physical training seriously and one of their own is appointed their PT director. All POWs get a 10 or 15-minute setting-up exercise right after morning roll call. Or the group may go for a brisk walk along the road for a round trip of a mile or two. Competitive sport, with basketball the most popular, helps pass the

Top: A PoW camp on the shores of the Yalu River.
Chinese People's Committee for World Peace

Above: There's nothing better than news from home when you're a PoW.
Chinese People's Committee for World Peace

Left: A Christmas 'party' in one of the PoW camps.
Chinese People's Committee for World Peace

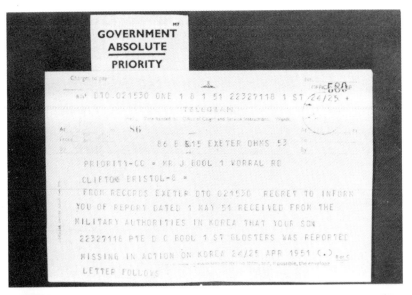

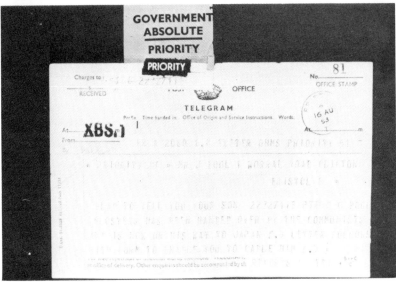

Above: 'Missing in action'. Families of soldiers in Korea must have dreaded receiving this sort of sudden news. . . But this time it ended happily. *Adam Forty*

time and keeps morale up. There are daily basketball, volleyball and soccer games. The sports and recreation committee keeps and active programme going for those less inclinded to muscle-flexing activities. Tournaments and championship playoffs in bridge, chess, checkers are available. Prizes of candy, apples and cigarettes go to the winners. A company championship playoff draws a large gallery and often side bets are made on the favourites. Cards are furnished, but the men have made their own chess figures and some sets representing many hours of wood-carving, are elaborate and show expert workmanship.''

Sounds marvellous doesn't it? Other articles in the same pamphlet have such titles as 'Plenty of Food', 'A healthy mind in a healthy body', 'A visitor from home' 'Medical Care', 'A Scrumptious Dinner' and 'POWs and families thank the China Peace Committee'. All the articles are liberally illustrated with photographs which show happy, well fed and contented POWs taking part in various activities in their camp. But are the smiles just a little too broad? Are the veritable mountains of food which the prisoners appear to be collecting and cooking *really* the sort of meals they actually received regularly? Was the treatment, the medical care, the sports and recreational facilities and all the rest really as good as this pamphlet endeavours to make out or is it all just a very clever and expertly put together piece of propaganda? Compare the article you have just read with this citation, taken from the London Gazette of 13 April 1954, for the award of the George Cross to Fusilier Derek Godfrey Kinne of the Royal Northumberland Fusiliers:

'In August 1950, Fusilier Kinne volunteered for service in Korea. He joined the 1st battalion, the Royal Northumberland Fusiliers, and was captured by Chinese Communist Forces on 25 April 1951, the last day of the Imjin River battle. From then on he had only two objects in mind: firstly to escape, and secondly by his contempt for his captors and their behaviour, and his utter disregard for the treatment meted out to him, to raise the morale of his fellow prisoners. The treatment which he received during his period of captivity is summarised in the succeeding paragraphs. Fusilier Kinne escaped for the first time within 24 hours of capture, but was retaken a few days later while attempting to regain our lines. Eventually he rejoined a large group of prisoners being marched north to the prison camps and, despite the hardships of this march which lasted a month, rapidly emerged as a man of outstanding leadership and very high morale. His conduct was a fine example to his fellow prisoners. In July 1952, Fusilier Kinne, who was now well known to his captors, was accused by them of being non-cooperative and was brutally interrogated about other POWs who had uncooperative views. As a result of his refusal to inform on his comrades, and for striking back at a Chinese officer who assaulted him, he was twice severely beaten up and tied up for periods of 12 and 24 hours, being made to stand on tip-toe with a running noose around his neck which would throttle him if he attempted to relax in any way. He escaped on 27 July, but was recaptured two days later. He was again beaten up very severely, and placed in handcuffs (which could be and frequently were tightened so as to restrict circulation), from which he was not released until 16 October 1952, a

149

period of 81 days. He was accused of insincerity, a hostile attitude towards the Chinese, "sabotage" of compulsory political study, escape and of being a reactionary. From 15 to 20 August he was confined in a very small box cell, where he was made to sit to attention all day, being periodically beaten, prodded with bayonets, kicked and spat upon by the guards, and denied any washing facilities. On 20 August 1952, he was made to stand to attention for seven hours and when he complained was beaten by the Chinese guard commander with the butt of a submarine gun, which eventually went off and killed the guard commander. For this Fusilier Kinne was beaten senseless with belts and bayonets, stripped of his clothes, and thrown into a dark, rat-infested hole until 19 September. He was frequently taken out and beaten, including once (on 16 September) with pieces of planking until he was unconscious. On 16 October, Fusilier Kinne was tried by a Chinese military court for escape and for being a reactionary and hostile to the Chinese, and was sentenced to 12 months' solitary confinement. This was increased to 18 months when he complained at his trial of denial of medical attention, including a double hernia which he had sustained in June 1952, while trying to escape.

'On 5 December 1952, he was transferred to a special penal company. His last award of solitary confinement was on 22 June 1953, when he was sentenced for defying Chinese orders and wearing a rosette in celebration of Coronation Day. He was eventually exchanged at Panmunjon on 10 August 1953. As late as 8 and 9 August he was threatened with non-repatriation for demanding an interview with the International Red Cross representatives who were visiting prisoner of war camps. Fusilier Kinne during the course of his periods of solitary confinement was kept in no less than seven different places of imprisonment, including a security police gaol, under conditions of the most extreme degradation and increasing brutality. Every possible method both physical and mental was employed by his captors to break his spirit, a task which proved utterly beyond their powers. Latterly he must have been fully aware that every time he flaunted his captors and showed openly his detestation of them and their methods he was risking his life. He was in fact several times threatened with death or non-repatriation. Nevertheless he was always determined to show that he was prepared neither to be intimidated nor cowed by brutal treatment at the hands of a barbarous enemy. His powers of

resistance and his determination to oppose and fight the enemy to the maximum, were beyond praise. His example was an inspiration to all ranks who came in contact with him.'

Francis Jones, in his evocative book *No Rice for Rebels*, tells the story of the capture and subsequent captivity of L Cpl R. F. Matthews BEM, of the REME attached to the Glosters, who was also captured during the Imjin battle. His story is very similar to that of Kinne, whom he met in the box-cells. These were large enough to allow a prisoner to sit down, but too short and too narrow for him to lie down in, except on his back with his knees sharply bent. The prisoners referred to their accommodation in these box-cells as 'The Kennel Club'. Throughout the book one gets a clear account of what life was really like in the camps, even for those who were not as uncooperative as Kinne and Matthews, and clearly a lack of proper facilities, of food and medical treatment was the norm. Another Gloster, Pte Dennis Bool, told me that after being captured in the Imjin battle, he and the other POWs had to march some 600 miles north to the prison camps. It took them 10 weeks and the route was over rough, mountainous terrain. He went on: 'After a 10-week march we arrived. We smelt the place — mud huts with no sanitation — before we saw it. Apart from having dysentery and bouts of malaria for the entire time I was there, I had toothache for six months until it was removed with a pair of pliers. During the summer we sawed wood, while the winters were a constant battle against

Left: Wounded SFC Richard Drozdowski of 2nd Recce, 2nd Infantry Division, was liberated by the Chinese after being taken captive and is helped by an Australian soldier Pte Roy Ingle from the village (in the background) where he had been held. *US Army photograph*

Above: An Australian soldier searching a North Korean captive near a burning North Korean farm, 26 October 1950. *UN (from US Army)*

the intense cold. Forty degrees of frost is no joke when you are inadequately clothed. The Chinese tried to indoctrinate us into their way of thinking, but without success. They were not too bad on the whole, although I did find myself in solitary for three weeks when an English-speaking interpreter overheard me saying that I would rather have died in battle if I'd known what I was to go through in that camp.' His proudest possession is a spoon he pinched from the back pocket of a well-fed guard during the march to the prison camp on the Manchurian border. Drummer Anthony Eagles was also taken in the same battle and remembers that during the journey north they were made to march all night and rest by day. Occasionally they were given millet and a type of barley called 'kaiolang'. Those who tried to escape were recaptured after a few days — he was free for six days before being retaken. Some were beaten when recaptured and many died owing to malnutrition, starvation, privations, torture and lack of medical facilities. His first 12 months of captivity were very rough, but conditions slowly improved once the peace talks started. He says: 'We had our moments though and refused to knuckle under to our captors and this was done in many ways; one was to have a sing-song each evening at dusk, finishing with "The King". When the Chinese objected to this, we asked if we could sing our second National Anthem, "Land of Hope and Glory". This seemed acceptable and became our National Anthem. I still get a lump in my throat when I hear this song.'

The day which Ex-POWs like Dennis Bool are never likely to forget came on 16 August 1953, when he walked across the 200-yard stretch of neutral ground that separated him from his Chinese captors and came to two immaculately dressed American policemen. 'OK, buddy, you're free,' they said as they escorted him towards the tents of Freedom Village. There were they first clean shaven white faces he had seen in two and a half years. A short identity parade was followed by a delousing session, a bucket shower, the issue of some clean clothes and an enormous meal. 'The sight of all these cold meats and rows and rows of chickens were too much for a mind in a 83lb body to comprehend', he reflected.

Of course it is difficult to generalise on the matter of POW treatment as it clearly varied not only from camp to camp, but also on what time in the war the men were taken prisoner. Brig C. N. Barclay includes a chapter on Commonwealth POWs in his history of the Division, in which he gives a

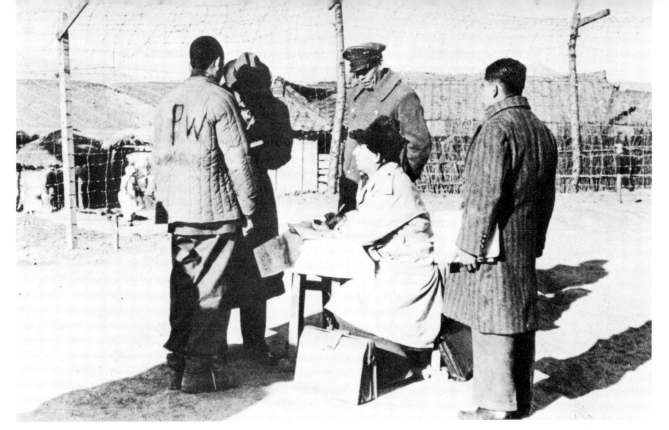

Above left: Men of the 24th Infantry Division round up Chinese prisoners during the fighting. *Soldier*

Left: A North Korean prisoner captured at Hoenjin on 18 October 1950. *UN*

Above: Interrogating a Chinese prisoner, December 1951. *UN*

description of POW life which is based upon a wide variety of statements, including one made by Col Carne VC, DSO of the Glosters. Clearly there are three distinct periods, the first being the early period in 1951, when nothing was properly organised, only the bare necessities of life were provided and the food was not only in short supply, but completely unsuitable for Europeans. Beri-beri became common, as well as other diseases due to vitamin deficiencies. Later in 1951 and on into 1952, POWs were more warmly clad and the food had improved, although it was still not anywhere near comparable with normal British or American diet. Accommodation was overcrowded and all comforts and amenities were non-existent. By the time most POWs were released in the late summer of 1953, conditions had been improved in many of the camps and were reasonably good for the average well-behaved POW. This was due undoubtedly to what was called the 'Lenient Policy' by which the Chinese hoped to persuade the prisoners to more readily accept Communist propaganda. At first this was carried out by a study programme of lectures and discussions, but when it did not produce many converts, more insidious ways of indoctrinating them were introduced, through books, papers and magazines — such as the one which I quoted at the start of this section. There was an immediate segregation of POWs by ranks on capture, and the Chinese actively discouraged any thrusting natural leaders among the rank and file — vide the treatment of Fusilier Kinne. Punishments were normally primitive, unpleasant and at times barbaric, although solitary confinement, prolonged interrogation and reduced diet, were the more normal ways rather than violent torture.

In 1973 the British Ministry of Defence published a pamphlet entitled *Treatment of British Prisoners of War in Korea*, in it the so-called 'Lenient Policy' is explained as is the Chinese technique of re-educating prisoners. This latter was what it was really all about, everything being designed to influence the thoughts of POWs and make them receptive to the Communist way of thinking. Those who were persuaded or pretended to be persuaded, could look forward to much improved treatment, while those who did not suffered accordingly and the harsh treatment meted out to them was explained away as merely being their own fault. One Chinese officer at Pyoktong in 1951 expressed this policy in a remark which must have sent shivers down the spines of all who heard him say: 'We will keep you here 10, 20, 30 or even 40 years if necessary, until you learn the truth, and if you still won't learn it, we will bury you so deep that you won't even stink.' Even the families of POWs were not left alone and an unrelenting campaign was waged against them by British Communists in UK. Many, for example, were harassed by members of the Communist run 'National Assembly of Women' to go to meetings and speak out against the war. One mother who had one son killed in Korea and another taken prisoner, regularly received leaflets. 'How many more sons have you got for the millionaires' fighting pool?' asked one in large red letters, which was pushed through her letterbox with a copy of the *Daily Worker*. Later she was visited by a woman from London and asked to go to speak at a meeting, but she didn't go. 'I know that some women who have been going to these meetings have been regularly receiving news from their boys,' she said, 'but it was 19 months before I heard from my son apart from a brief note to say he was a POW. I was told it was probably because he was refusing to cooperate with the Reds.'

Prisoners of the UN Command

It would be nice to be able to report that, unlike the UN soldiers who were taken prisoner, their counterparts in the camps in South Korea received the very best of treatment. Unfortunately, there was a good deal of trouble in some of the camps, although some of it was deliberately stirred up by the POWs themselves in order to produce good propaganda material for the world's press. Probably the most well known and largest incident occurred on 7 May 1952 on the offshore island of Koje — a rocky inhospitable island off the south coast near Pusan, where a POW camp had been established some months after the Chinese intervention in the war. By the end of 1951, there were over 130,000 North Koreans and 20,000 Chinese POW on the island, in enormous compounds of about 5,000 each, under a mixed guard of American and South Korean military police. Although the Americans managed to screen out nearly 40,000 of these captives as being South Koreans, the remaining POWs started to organise resistance against the authorities. There was evidence that this unrest was organised and directed from North Korea — radio sets and elaborate message passing chains were later uncovered, whilst Communist organisers set up

'kangaroo courts' to punish POWs who tried to take advantage of further screening. Soon riots were commonplace and in February 1952 a battalion of US infantry had to be used to maintain order in one compound during a screening operation. Using home-made weapons, the prisoners attacked the soldiers, killing one and wounding 38. The troops opened fire, inflicting over 200 casualties. Thereafter the POWs were virtually masters of their compounds, while the guards could do no more than stay outside, under orders not to use force. The climax came on 7 May 1952, (which incidentally coincided with the arrival in the theatre of the newly appointed Supreme Commander, Gen Mark W. Clark) when the prisoners seized the Camp Commander, Brig-Gen F. T. Dodd, while he was talking to them at the gate of their compound. His successor, Brig C. F. Colson, was presented with a long series of demands, which implied American brutality and coercion, to which he had to agree in order to gain Dodd's freedom, thus giving the Communist peace negotiators at Panmunjon some marvellous 'ammunition' to use against the United Nations. Although Gen Clark later repudiated everything, as it had occurred under the threat of coercion, the damage had been done — 'the biggest flap of the whole war' was the way Gen Clark described it. The world's press had a field day, as charges and countercharges were flung back and forth at Panmunjon, although Gen Clark quickly replaced both Dodd and Colson, sent in a capable field commander (Brig H. L. Boatner) to take charge and made the guard force a UN commitment.

Repatriation

The repatriation of prisoners took place in two phases. First of all, in late April 1953 Operation 'Little Switch' was staged at Panmunjon when a total of 6,670 sick and disabled Communists were exchanged for just 684 allied prisoners. Operation 'Big Switch' did not take place until after the armistice had been signed, when 75,823 Chinese and North Koreans were exchanged for 3,597 allied POWs. Of course there were also a number of 'nonrepatriates', those who chose to stay either north or south of the 38th Parallel when the exchange was made. The total still held by UN Command were 14,704 Chinese and 7,900 North Koreans, while 335 South Koreans, 23 Americans and one British serviceman chose to stay with their captors. Perhaps these figures alone will say far more than I could ever hope to about the success (or otherwise) of the Communist attempts at indoctrination.

Below: Carrying ROK flags, North Korean PoWs who chose to stay in South Korea, board a 'Freedom Train', 21 January 1954.
Public Archives Canada

The armistice is signed

At 1000 on 27 July 1953, after two years and 17 days of armistice negotiations, which had amounted to 575 regular meetings and 18 million words, the Korean Armistice Agreement was signed, thus ending the longest truce talks in world history! They were signed by the local chief delegates of both sides at Panmunjon, in an atmosphere of unparalleled chill and unfriendliness. The ceremony took place in a huge barn-like structure called 'Hall of Peace', made of wood and bamboo, which the Communists had knocked together in three days. Originally the gables had been adorned with Picasso-like peace doves, but these were removed after UN protests. Inside, there was rigid segregation as though an iron curtain divided the room, with UN representatives and world press on one side, Communists and their press representatives on the other. Along the centre of the hall were three long tables, with the United Nations and Korean flags at opposite ends. At exactly 1000 Gen Harrison and Gen Nam II, entered from opposite ends and without any sign of recognition of each other's presence, proceeded to separate tables. Aides started to place the 36 copies of the Armistice in front of them. English versions were bound in blue, Chinese in red and North Korean in white. They signed in complete silence and when they had finished, both stood up and walked outside, still without any sign of recognition to their opposite number. Gen Mark Clark countersigned the documents at Munsan in the presence of numerous UN representatives. 'We have stopped the shooting' he said '. . . therefore I am thankful. It is, however, only a step towards what must yet be done. The task is now to put the cease-fire into full effect as quickly

Below: Tanks of 3rd US Infantry Division prepare to leave their positions following the signing of the armistice, on 29 July 1953. *US Army*

as we can and get down to working out an enduring settlement of the Korean problem. I cannot find it in me to exult in this hour. Rather, it is a time for prayer that we may succeed in our particularly difficult endeavour to turn the armistice to the advantage of mankind. If we extract hope from this occasion it must be diluted with recognition that our salvation requires unrelaxing vigilance and effort'. Twelve hours after the signing, the guns were silenced on the front lines and the troops began to fall back behind the four-kilometre wide buffer zone.

The ceasefire ended 37 months of hostilities in the course of which it has been estimated that 72,500 United Nations forces had been killed, and more than 250,000 wounded. Some 84,000 others had been captured or were missing. Of the dead, 25,000 were from the United States, 600 British, 1,900 other UN forces and 45,000 South Koreans. In addition the tiny country of South Korea had been ravaged by the war and an estimated 600,000 homes had been destroyed and 10 million people had endured great hardship. At one time there were up to five million refugees being cared for by the United Nations Command. On the other side a total of about 1,350,000 North Koreans and Chinese had been killed or wounded. Throughout the war the US Eighth Army had coped with a great deal more than just

the fighting front. It had, for example, trained and outfitted the ROK Army and most other UN forces; operated its own logistical command; provided food, clothing and medical relief for millions of refugees; supplied military advisory personnel and established a military school system for the ROK Army; supported both the Air Force and the Marines logistically; extended and improved the Korean road system; transported all of its own supplies, ammunition and personnel replacements to the battlefronts, mostly from the port of Pusan, 300 miles to the south; supplied technical advisers and aid to several ROK government ministries; helped in the rehabilitation of Korean agriculture, fisheries, manufacturing and mining, with supplies and equipment, transport, advisory services and finance. Gen Ridgway paid tribute to his men thus: '... unsurpassed standards ... in professional competence, fidelity, loyalty, courage and spiritual stamina ... It was this command with these qualities, which challenged, met and hurled back the most vicious forces which have yet threatened mankind in its age-old struggle to gain and preserve the dignity and freedom of the individual. I believe it quite possible that because of this action history may someday record that the crest of the Communist wave of cold blooded aggression was broken against the arms and the will

Below: 'Take me back to dear old Blighty!' Men of 1 DWR on the dockside at Pusan, as they board the HMT Asturias at the end of their tour in Korea, 13 November 1953.
RHQ DWR

to fight of the United Nations battle team in Korea; and that this menacing flood, reaching its high water mark on the Korean front, thereafter began its recession in Asia'.

Korea today

So ended the Korean War, waged in the remote 'Land of the Morning Calm'. The Republic of South Korea had been rescued by an international command, led by the United States of America and spearheaded by the Eighth Army. By no stretch of the imagination could it be said that they had achieved a great victory, but rather an uneasy armed truce. Twenty seven years later the situation has not really altered. No peace treaty has yet been signed, and, although the major fighting stopped with the signing of the armistice, the North continues its acts of aggression against the South, as though trying to goad them into yet another full scale war. It is worth noting that the armed forces of the Democratic People's Republic of North Korea rank as the fourth largest in the Communist world. They are well equipped, well trained and aggressive in outlook. On the other side of the 38th Parallel the United Nations Command has remained in being; however, the vast majority of nations speedily withdrew their respective components once the armistice had been signed. Now all that remains of these

fighting forces are those of the United States (much reduced) and of the Republic of Korea. South Korea was, as already explained, terribly devastated by the war, its economy was in ruins, many of its people homeless, jobless, starving and dispirited. It took some years and a lot of help from the USA to improve the situation. Since 1962, the ROK has undertaken a programme of economic growth which must be the envy of most other countries in the world. While production in nations such as our own has been going steadily downhill, South Korea has maintained a staggering average real growth rate of 9.3% of its gross national product. But economic growth has not been the only development. The ROK armed forces have also expanded and are undoubtedly now a force to be reckoned with, their strength, weaponry and capabilities being almost on a par with their belligerent northern neighbour. (The armed forces of North Korea were estimated in 1979-80 to be about 650,000, while those in the South were almost 620,000.) Their increased efficiency has been recognised; for example, in 1971, South Korean troops replaced American in ground positions along the DMZ (Demilitarised Zone) north of Seoul, and a combined corps headquarters was established to control the Korean and American forces guarding the DMZ. The primary mission of this command which is

Below: Men of 1 DWR move up the gangway on board the troopship HMT *Asturias*.
RHQ DWR

now known as the Combined Forces Command (CFC), is to deter and, if necessary, to repel any external armed attack. The CFC contains, as the main US Army ground element, the 2nd US Infantry Division. There is ample evidence that their presence in South Korea is very necessary, indeed the large and growing offensive threat from the North recently halted US plans to withdraw numbers of their troops. Commando-type raids, tunnelling under the UN Command sector of the DMZ, active clandestine infiltrations by sea and land — clearly the CFC must continually ensure that its troops are fit to fight and determined to do so. In addition to 2nd Infantry Division, the USA retains an Air Defence Artillery Brigade in Korea, who scan the skies from their mountain missile sites, while a Support Command provides everything the fighting troops need to function. As Gen John A. Wickham Jr, commander of US Forces in Korea, wrote at the end of an article in the October 1979 issue of *Army* magazine: All Eighth Army soldiers and other members of the US forces in Korea do their jobs quietly, professionally and willingly in the knowledge that they contribute to keeping the peace on the Korea peninsula. Peace and stability in this region remain inextricably linked to US national security interests'. It is good to know that at least some people in the West have such a firm resolve. Those who fought for the principles of the United Nations in the Korean War must surely echo his sentiments.

Above: Dockside service for Greek soldiers killed in Korea, whose bodies have been shipped home.
Greek Embassy

Left: Even after the armistice, the Peace Commission continued its work. This meeting was held in November 1968, after a North Korean seaborne commando raid into the south. Maj-Gen H. Woodward, US Army, is making a statement, while Maj-Gen Park Chung Kuk, left of picture, listens.
Brig A. D. R. G. Wilson

Right: Men of the 25th Canadian Infantry Brigade bid farewell to their fallen comrades before returning to Canada, at the United Nations Cemetery Pusan, 23 April 1953.
Public Archives Canada

Bibliography

Appleman, Roy E.; *US Army in the Korean War, South to the Naktong, north to the Yalu*; Office of the Chief of Military History, US Army, 1961.

Barclay, Brig C. N.; *The First Commonwealth Division*; Gale & Polden, 1954.

Barker, Lt-Col A. J.; *Fortune Favours the Brave*; Leo Cooper Ltd, 1974.

Bartlett, Norman (ed); *With the Australians in Korea*; Thomas Nelson and Sons Ltd, 1952.

Carew, Tim; *Korea, the Commonwealth at War*; Cassell, 1967.

David, Capt Allan A. (ed); *Battleground Korea*; 25th Infantry Division Council, 1951.

Futrell, Robert Frank; *The US Air Force in Korea*; Duell, Sloan and Pearce, 1961.

Gugeler, Russell A.; *Combat Actions in Korea*; Office of the Chief of Military History US Army, 1970.

Harding, Col E. D.; *The Imjin Roll*; Barton Press Ltd, 1976.

Hermes Walter, G.; *US Army in the Korean War, Truce Tent and Fighting Front*; Office of the Chief of Military History, US Army, 1966.

Jones, Francis S.; *No Rice for Rebels*; The Bodley Head, 1956.

Malcolm, Lt-Col G. I.; *The Argylls in Korea*; Thomas Nelson and Sons Ltd, 1952.

Marshall, Brig-Gen S. L. A.; *The Military History of the Korean War*; Franklin Watts Inc, 1963.

Montross, Lyn and Canzona, Capt Nicholas A. USMC; *US Marine Operations in Korea 1950-53, The Inchon-Seoul Operation*; Historical Branch HQ USMC, 1955.

Munroe, Lt Clark C.; *The Second Infantry Division in Korea 1950-51*; Toppan Printing Co, Tokyo.

Oliver, Robert T.; *The Truth about Korea*; Putnam & Co Ltd, 1951.

Sawyer, Maj Robert K.; *Military Advisors in Korea: KMAG in peace and war*; Office of the Chief of Military History, US Army, 1962.

Thomas, Maj R. C. W.; *The War In Korea*; Gale & Polden, 1954.

Wood, Lt-Col Herbert Fairlie; *Strange Battleground, the official history of the Canadian Army in Korea*; Crown copyright, Ottawa, 1966.

Official publications

Ministry of Defence, London: *Treatment of British Prisoners in Korea*; HMSO.

United Nations Department of Public Information: *How the United Nations met the challenge in Korea*; UN Publications, 1953.

United Nations POW's in Korea; Chinese People's Committee for World Peace, Peking, 1953.

The War History Compilation Committee: *The History of the United Nations Forces in the Korean War, Volumes 1 to 5 inclusive*; The Ministry of National Defense, the Republic of Korea, 1972-76.

Regimental Periodicals

The Back Badge; The Journal of the Gloucestershire Regiment.

The Iron Duke; The Journal of the Duke of Wellington's Regiment.

The Korean Journal of the First Royal Tank Regiment 1952-53.